MW01290706

BECOMING

— A —

SECOND
MILE

— LEADER

Excel at
exceeding
expectations.

Jon Ashcraft

BECOMING A SECOND MILE LEADER

Copyright © 2018 Jon Ashcraft

All rights reserved. No part of this publication may be repro-
duced, stored in a retrieval system, or transmitted in any form or
by any means, electronic, mechanical, photocopying, recording,
scanning, or otherwise, except as permitted under Section 107 or
108 of the 1976 United States Copyright Act, without the prior
written permission of the publisher.

Printed in the United States of America
First Printing, 2018

ISBN -13:978-1086242386
ISBN -10:1086242386

Blazing Star Publishing
6109 Fairmont Parkway
Pasadena, TX 77505

Jon Ashcraft
www.facebook.com/jonashcraft
instagram.com/jawaba

Art Direction: Amy Smith Design
www.linkedin.com/in/Amy-SmithDesign

PRAISE FOR BECOMING A SECOND MILE LEADER

WARNING: Don't read this book unless you are willing to be challenged, charged and convinced of a Christian Disciple-making mandate. I believe THE SECOND MILE is a must-read for every Church member and every church leader who wants to move beyond the "status quo" of Churchianity into the realm of disciple-making ministry. This book has the potential to transform church congregations from introverted social groups to explosive soul-winning, discipling, world-changing Kingdom builders!
- Larry Pyle, Dmin

Becoming a Second Mile Leader is more than a book about "methods" to lead the local church into significance and impact. This book is about "ethos" — the characteristic culture of a church manifested in its values, beliefs and most importantly, its actions. Jon Ashcraft is giving voice and vocabulary to those of us in church ministry that want to awaken the sleeping giant of ministers and ministries within our congregation. If you are ready for a reformation in your local church, this book is a good place to start.
- Thomas T. Hale - Multiplier, Ron Cottle Ministries

With practical and personal stories to illustrate every point, Becoming a Second-Mile Leader is an enjoyable read with a transformational revival of Biblical leadership for the New Testament Church. Jon Ashcraft wrote a book with the solution Leaders have in their hearts & hope for the people they influence. Becoming a Second-Mile Leader is Jesus' mandate that will take a congregation full of potential and turn it into a Church of productivity! You cannot read this book without developing a better vision for leading the Body of Christ to make a bigger impact in their world.

     - Pastor Chris Frye, New Hope Eunice, La (EuniceChurch. com)

     Jon Ashcraft is a faithful man who has been fully engaged in following Jesus for the 20+ years I've known him. He has served in just about every aspect of ministry. Jon gets it. His take on the church is refreshing, challenging and inspires me to keep giving myself to the hope of the world, the church of Jesus.

     - E. Wayne Drain, Founding Pastor of Fellowship of Christians and co-author of *He Still Speaks.*

THANK YOU

To my wife, Aimee Ashcraft. You are the strongest and smartest woman I know. You are full of wisdom, grace and poise, taking on the most complex and difficult challenges. You handled the being a mom, a pastor, a counselor, a financier and business manager while I just tried to figure out what to type in this book. You do all the heavy lifting and allow me to excel in life because of your support. This book would not be possible without you. You are the epitome of a Second Mile Leader. I am thankful for your constant encouragement and faithful friendship. You are the best part of the two of us.

To my parents, Robert and Ida Ashcraft. I have no idea who I would be without your guidance, fervent prayer, and the example of your lives. You imparted a Godly heritage, a foundation of faith, and a multi-generational anointing into my life. Thank you for all your sacrifices, all the times you prayed for me, and all the love you gave me. I am who I am because of you.

To Pastor Don Nordin. Thank you for believing in me enough to give me a chance to lead a campus through CT Church. I am honored to serve the vision you paid so much to see become a reality. Thank you for stretching me to do more than I think I can do. Thank you for challenging me to put my leadership teachings in book form. Any fruit that comes from this book will be because of your encouragement and challenge.

To Larry and Georgiann Pyle. I thank God you became my spiritual parents, not simply my parents-in-law. I learned what the church really was because of what you taught me. Many ideas within these pages are yours. Thank you for showing me the church is not a building, but a people with a purpose. Thank you for writing those ideas in your book, Stop Going To Church, The Dynamics of Being the Church. You gave me language to help put these lessons into book form. Your legacy lives on through those you raised in the faith.

FOREWORD

Becoming A Second Mile Leader, written by Jon Ashcraft, contains some of the best material available for training lay leaders. My first comment to Jon when he introduced me to this course was, "You must to get this material into a format that can be easily utilized by pastors and church leaders."

Over the past year, Susan and I have used this material to raise up more than 100 Second Mile Leaders at CT Church's main campus. The results have been astonishing! We are currently in the most dramatic season of church growth we have seen in 17 years. I credit this to the Second Mile Leaders training. Each Sunday morning at the end of our service Susan and I stand at the front of the auditorium and greet those who are new to the church and I would say that more than 90 percent have been brought to church by a Second Mile Leader.

We require our Second Mile Leaders to be a home opener, to host, or at the minimum to assist with a life group. The life groups the Second Mile Leaders oversee are growing exponentially. The greatest thing is that these leaders are also bringing those new people to Sunday services. Because of the efforts of the Second Mile Leaders, these folks are getting plugged into the life of the church and disciples are being made. Currently, more than 80 percent of our Sunday morning attendees are part of a life group some time during the week! Isn't this what Jesus commanded us to do? If my memory serves me correctly, He said, "Go make disciples!" Second Mile Leadership is a disciple-making process! It ends the "Come and see" mentality, and initiates the "Go and make disciples" process.

Second Mile Leadership is not for everyone. Some people are too traditionally religious to submit to the process. Others are too rebellious to endure the process. The first thing I say to each group of potential Second Mile Leaders is this: "This class is not for everyone! If at any point you realize you cannot commit to what we are asking of you, you may exit the room at the break and not come back. I can still be your pastor and you can still attend this church but unless you can commit to the entire process I cannot endorse you as a Second Mile Leader!"

Those who complete the process are never the same! They are loyal followers of their leaders and become do-or-die disciples!

I wholeheartedly endorse this book and recommend that every pastor and disciple maker read it and consider implementing it in your ministry.

- Don Nordin, Lead Pastor CT Church

CONTENTS

INTRODUCTION... 10

READING GUIDE 15

THE SECOND MILE.. 17

WHAT IS THE CHURCH? 22

IT'S NOT ABOUT ME.. 42

EVERY BELIEVER A MINISTER 65

IT'S UP TO ME 84

MULTIPLY MINISTRY 102

RENTERS VERSUS OWNERS 123

CIRCLES ARE BETTER THAN ROWS 140

WE DON'T GET TO GET WHAT WE WANT.................... 161

THE FOUR C'S 176

WATCH YOUR ATTITUDE...................................... 195

MAKING DISCIPLES 218

A SHEPHERD'S HEART 237

RELATIONAL CURRENCY 256

LEADING WITH AN OPEN HEART 275

ARE YOU FAT? 295

LEADERSHIP COVENANTS.................................... 315

INTRODUCTION

I have an irrational fear of water. It comes from an experience I had as a small child. In fact, I was so small I don't even remember it happening. Our family was camping with some friends on a lake in Arkansas. Some of them decided it was time for me to learn how to swim, so they threw me in. I was thrown in to sink or swim. I sank.

I probably would have figured out how to swim if I had been left alone for a bit longer, but my Momma loves me. She screamed at those mean old men and made them scoop me up from the water. They saved me from drowning. Since I never learned to swim, however, I have had an intense fear of water.

I have since learned how to swim, but I've never conquered my fear of the water. If you put me in a swimming pool where I can easily reach the sides or sink to the bottom and push myself back to the top, I am OK. If you put me in a boat, I make sure I know where the life jackets are. I usually do not jump out and swim while everyone else does. The underlying fear of the water causes me to panic when I get into a situation that I can't control.

This happened recently on a vacation. I was having fun at a water park with my family. There were waterslides, zip lines, wave pools, and lazy rivers. I normally have no issues at water parks because I'm 6' 5" and the water is usually four or five feet deep. Swimming is not necessary. Standing is all that is needed.

We decided to go down a waterslide. This normally is no problem for me; I hit the water and stand up. When I hit the water on this particular slide, however, I tumbled and became disoriented. The water was very murky, so I could not see which way was up or down.

I thought to myself that I would just put my legs down and stand up. When I did, there was no bottom within reach. I started to swim, thinking I was swimming up to the surface of the pool; however, I was not breaking the surface of the water. I could not figure out what was going on, and panic started to set in. I thought this might be the end.

I felt a hand grab my arm to help me. The lifeguard had come to pull me out. I was so disoriented and panicked I still could not tell what was going on. I finally relaxed enough for the lifeguard to help me get oriented. I stood up. The water was waist deep.

Apparently I had been trying to swim to the surface, not realizing my body was in a horizontal position. I had nearly drowned in waist-deep water. I sheepishly walked to the side of the pool where my oldest daughter was waiting for me. She was confused at what happened. I did not explain, and I did not go down any more water-slides that day.

I still haven't talked to my family about this. It is embarrassing to write it in this book actually. I should know better. I should do better. It is crazy to think I could have drowned in water that was only waist-deep. I had the ability to stand and walk out of my situation. I just could not figure out how to do it.

I believe this is a parallel to the church in the United States.

Church leaders find themselves floundering, trying to stay afloat. Lack of volunteers makes weekend services an event to dread rather than welcome. Budget hurdles make leading difficult. Vision is cut off from provision. There is much to be done to move the church forward, but many leaders find themselves navigating crisis after crisis.

I have been part of church staff and ministry since 1992. In that time, I have never found a pastor or leader who is wanting to do less. The vision to do more never goes away. As long as Heaven and Hell are realities, we must figure out ways to do more to bring people out of darkness and into the light of God's Kingdom.

Yet many times we find ourselves frustrated, unable to move to have a mass effect on society due to lack of resources, leaders, and finances.

We know the local church is the hope of the world. Yet it seems we often have little effect. While we are very busy, it seems our society around us continues to crumble in moral decay. Why?

I believe there is a parallel between my water park experience and our church leadership. We are working hard. We are giving it everything we have, but for many pastors it is simply not working. Yet, just as I had the ability to walk out of the water, I believe we are very capable of changing our local churches. We just don't realize it.

The church that Jesus left on the Earth radically changed the world in just a few years. They had very few resources, were very unpopular with the established religions of the day, and faced tremendous persecution. Yet they persisted and radically changed the cultural landscape in just a few years. What did they have that we do not? What has changed from then until now?

Today we have church leaders giving it all they have. Good church leaders are not lazy. Most are disciplined and driven by a dream to change the world. They are passionate about what they do. They are leading just as I was swimming. Yet emotionally, spiritually, and physically spent, they are nearing the point where they want to give up.

Why aren't our churches moving forward? If the disciples that Jesus left could so radically reshape the world with the Great Commission and the power of the Holy Spirit, why not us?

The mind-set of the early church regarding what a Christian and a church should be shifted during church history. Ideas are powerful. They have the ability to propel us forward or set us back. Unfortunately these mind-sets have done the latter.

When I became pastor of a church in Houston, Texas, I realized I needed to tackle some of these paradigms head-on. To be able to change our church to reach its full potential, I needed to present some scriptural truths in a way that would destroy these crippling mind-sets. I developed a course of study I called "Second Mile Leaders." It was a course of teachings that I took my leadership team through in order to open our eyes and reorient us around that original purpose. This book is the compilation of those teachings.

I'm sure it is incomplete and leaves many stones unturned; however, the leaders that have taken this course of study have become key players in the reformation of our church. We have seen a radical transformation in the level of ownership of the vision of our church. We have seen lay leaders come alive to purpose and the dream of God for their lives for the local church.

If you are member of a local church body, I pray the concepts in this book awaken you to your God-given purpose. If you are a leader in the church, I pray these concepts ring true. I hope you are able to use them to help your church understand what God desires for and from them while they are in this world.

READING GUIDE

This book is laid out in the format in which it was presented to our leaders. We met with our leaders for 8 weeks and presented concepts to them to help mobilize them into ministry.

Each week contained two topics. One dealt with the Biblical view and philosophy of the church, along with a cursory glance at church history. This first lesson would lay a foundation about what the church should look like.

The second lesson dealt with attitudes of the heart. It was intended to help align the hearts of our leaders toward the purposes of God in the church in the world. The topic made the leaders look inward to decide if they were willing to take the challenge of what it means to be a Second Mile Leader.

Each week one lesson would be informational; the second would be inspirational. The first dealt with the head; the second dealt with the heart.

It is helpful to have this information at the outset of your reading so you will understand what is happening as you read this book. Each pair of chapters represents a week of teaching that was presented in the class. Two parallel tracks are presented with each set of two chapters and can be visualized as follows:

Information: Chapter 1. What Is The Church?

Inspiration: Chapter 2. It's Not About You

In essence this is two books in one with each laying a different foundation. As you read, you will notice it seems we switch back and forth between ideas with each chapter. Hopefully this will help you navigate the pages ahead and help the ideas connect more powerfully.

I pray that this inspires and motivates you to do and be all that God wants within the context of the local church. As his body, we are the only hope this world has. It is time to become the body of Christ on a mission, Second Mile Leaders. Let's get started.

THE SECOND MILE

If a soldier demands that you carry his gear
for a mile, carry it two miles.
- Jesus (Matthew 5:41 NLT)

Imagine a foreign government overtaking the United States. They strip away every liberty you have ever experienced. Your rights are removed. All you have known until this time in your life is no more. The ruling government has taken control of your life. What would your attitude toward that government be? Resentful? Rebellious? Of course!

This is the situation the Jews found themselves in when Jesus arrived. Rome had occupied their territory. A foreign government was dictating tax, law, and religious freedom. The Jews would have loved nothing more than to see an uprising to overthrow this government and see their nation restored to its rightful place as God's chosen people.

During their occupation of Israel, the Roman soldiers could lawfully conscript any Jew into temporary service. Regardless of the interruption or the inconvenience, Roman officials and soldiers could make certain legal demands on the citizens over which they ruled.

One of these laws allowed Roman soldiers to compel a Jew

to carry a soldier's gear. If he needed help or was tired, he could demand a citizen pick up his equipment and carry it for him.

Imagine the insult. You have lost your freedoms. You are subject to a pagan nation. To add insult to injury, this soldier has the right to enlist your service. He can rightfully interrupt your day and further humiliate you by making you carry his gear. As the Abingdon Creative Preaching Annual 2014 states:

> *The Romans had a law by which they could make their subjects carry a soldier's gear for one mile. This is what allowed the Romans to make Simon of Cyrene carry Jesus' cross (Mark 15:21). Pressing Jews into service was widely practiced throughout the country—and widely resented.[1]*

The "mile" in those days was measured by 1000 steps. The Jews held to the letter of the law on this. At exactly 1000 steps, they dropped the soldier's pack. They refused to do more than the minimum.

As Jesus began his ministry to the public, he launched into his keynote address, the Sermon on the Mount. At first the people were probably agreeable to the topics. He told them how they would be blessed. So far so good.

Then Jesus began to ratchet up commitment and expectation. He began saying things like, "You have heard it said, but *I* say to you."

The pleasant platitudes were gone. Jesus went further than

the letter of the law. He moved beyond the actions of sin and confronted the seat of sin—the heart. He makes it even harder to be self-righteous as He proclaimed that it is the *thoughts*, not the *actions*, that are sinful.

In one of these statements, He referred to this resented Roman law that allowed the soldiers to force them to carry their gear. As He began the statement, "If a soldier demands that you carry his gear," they were likely hoping that Jesus would give them permission to rebel against the Romans, telling them to "buzz off," "take a hike," or "do it yourself."

Yet what Jesus said to finish the statement was unthinkable. He told them that when they were forced to carry a pack for one mile, the legal limit, to carry it voluntarily a second mile!

Imagine the outrage, the murmurs, and whispers. The people were looking for a messiah, a savior—not only to save them from their sins but also to save them from this government. They hoped for a leader with enough charisma that everyone would fall in line and do whatever it took to throw off the constraints of this illegal occupation. Just as they thought Jesus might say something that would instigate a riot and start a rebellion, He let them down. Instead of appealing to their resentment and hatred, instead of working them up into a rebellious frenzy, he let all the wind out of their sails.

A compliant body does not indicate an aligned heart.

Jesus said, "Don't just do the minimum, double it." Do more than you're asked or can be commanded. Go above and beyond. Do the unexpected. Go the second mile.

Jesus does this every single time. He acknowledges the minimum (the law) but asks his followers to go beyond it. He asks them to have more than right *behavior*. He asks them to have the right *heart*.

For years Aimee and I have done our best to parent for our children's hearts. While we knew we could force their behavior, something deeper needed to be fixed. We knew that we could force them to sit down, ground them, or take away privileges, and we have done *all* those things. Yet while our children may have been sitting down on the outside, they were standing up on the inside. A compliant body does not indicate an aligned heart.

Children with hearts that are in rebellion must be restrained by some external control. We knew that without parenting for the heart, the moment our children were out of our sight they would do what they wanted in the first place.

Of course Jesus knows this better than we do. This is why he makes our obedience about our hearts, not our actions. This is why he upended their expectations and asked them to do double instead of nothing. Jesus doesn't want children who do the minimum. He wants people to know not just the law, but the *lawgiver*. He wants our heart. Once He has our heart, our behavior will follow.

How can we turn the other cheek? How can we give our cloak when only our shirt is demanded? How can we love our enemies? How can we *willingly* go the second mile? It can happen only when our hearts are aligned with His heart.

Have you limited your love to someone in your life? Have

you cut people out of your circle because they are too difficult? Do you ignore the call to serve in your church because you're "too busy" when truthfully it is laziness or selfishness? Are you characterized by doing the minimum? Do you live a life of service to God and show love to others around you that is "good enough"? If so, maybe it's time to check your heart to see if it is aligned with Jesus.

Many of us are guilty of doing the minimum–for our spouses, our jobs, and the church. We reveal our hearts as we seek to know the exact minimum standard for our behaviors and expectations. We want to be able to check the boxes next to each of them and go on to whatever it is that we *really* care about.

If you find yourself doing the minimum and calling that good, perhaps it is time you had a meaningful conversation with your Savior and see if there is a need for open heart surgery–the kind that will make you willingly do more than is required or even asked for your boss, spouse, family, pastor, and church. Maybe it's time for you to go the second mile.

WHEN YOU LOVE WITHOUT LIMITS, YOU LOVE LIKE GOD.

1

WHAT IS THE CHURCH?

Upon this rock I will build my church,
and all the powers of hell will not conquer it.
- Jesus (Matthew 16:18 NLT)

Think of your church for a moment. What drew you to it? What's your favorite thing about it? Is it acts of service in the community? Evangelism? Is it a discipleship program that you love? Perhaps the weekend services are your favorite part.

If you were to share your excitement about your church with a coworker or friend and extend an invitation, how would you describe its location? Would you reference it by street intersection, such as "the corner of Main and Broadway?" Would you describe it in proximity to a popular store or landmark? Perhaps you would say, "It is across from the outlet mall," or "next door to the post office." Or would you simply give the physical address so someone could find it by using the maps application on their phone?

Any number of these methods would work for giving a physical description of your church. Yet none of those descriptions would be fully accurate descriptions regarding the location of your church.

The Church Is Not A *Place*. The Church Is A *People*!

While your directions and descriptions would help someone find the location where your church meets for services, trainings, and other activities, it is not the location of the church itself. The reason is simple. The building is not the church. The church is the people who gather *in* it.

If you were to ask me where my church is at this moment, I could not give you an answer. I might know where *some* of my church is, but not all of it. At this moment, they are in various locations throughout the Houston area. The only way I could accurately describe the location of my church would be if every member were assembled in one place with no one missing. If we could manage to do that (and we never do), then I could tell you the exact location of my church. The remainder of the time, I have no way to describe accurately the location of my church because I simply do not know where all of them are.

The Church Is Not A Place. The Church Is A People.

When we say the word "church," the first thing that typically comes to mind is some*thing*, not some*one*. We think of the building where we meet. Yet the church is not a *place*; the church is a *people*! If someone were to say to you, "Hey, let's go to church this weekend," they would be asking you to do something that is actually impossible. You cannot *go* to church because you *are* the church!

This may come as no surprise to you. It it not a new concept. We have known this for years. Maybe you did not even fall for my trick above in describing the location. Yet when we use the word "church," we are usually referring to the physical location of the building. Why is it when someone uses the word "church," our minds immediately visualize the place our church meets?

The language we use to describe the church has conditioned us to think of it as a building. Words are powerful tools. They create images and ideas. These ideas influence our behaviors. Repeated behaviors become entrenched, and patterns of prompt and response are ingrained. As soon as we are prompted with certain words, our minds react, creating the associated images and ideas we have come to understand experientially. Almost without thinking, our mental programming produces a set of behaviors that aligns with our experiential truth. Right or wrong, we are trapped in our way of doing things.

Without accurate language to frame our understanding, things lose their significance and purpose. I believe this explains much of the problem in the church today. We have misunderstood what church means or is supposed to be. We do not know why it exists or what it does. We are locked into ideas that are a misunderstanding of God's purpose and intention for the church. We continue to do what we have always done with little or no thought as to if this is what we *should* be doing.

Zig Ziglar tells a story about a woman who sends her husband to the store to purchase a ham. "After he bought it, she asked him why he failed to have the butcher cut off the end of the ham. [The husband] asked his wife why she wanted him to cut off the end. She replied that her mother had always done it that way and that was reason enough for her. Since the wife's mother was visiting, they asked her why she always cut off the end of the ham. The mother replied that this was the way *her* mother did it. Mother, daughter, and [the husband] then decided to call grandmother and solve this three-generation mystery. Grandmother promptly replied that she cut the end off the ham because her roaster was too small to cook it in one piece."[2]

This story illustrates so well how we can become stuck in methods, thinking, and behaviors without a second thought as to whether this is what we should be doing. We never question if there was a reason someone *started* doing it that way and if we should continue doing it that way.

Not What We Have Always Done

Our language regarding the church has shaped our culture and behaviors. Without much thought, we continue in our pattern of behavior. We "go to church" because it is what we have always done. We bring our Bibles, dress in our Sunday best, sing songs, and listen to the preacher. We leave, head to lunch, go home, and prepare for "real life" in the "real world." Just like the woman who cut the end off the ham, we assume since this is what mom and dad did, it is what every generation before them has done as well. Yet this is not what the church has always been, and it is not what the church has always done.

Jesus Did Not Build A Church

The early church was very different from the one we see today. It was a group of people so dedicated to the cause of Christ that they would risk beatings, imprisonment, and even death to be associated with the name of Jesus.

What understanding would be so strong that the early followers would endure so much suffering and scorn to follow Jesus and advance His cause? They had a clear picture of what Jesus wanted them to be. They knew what He meant when He said he was going to build His church. The word Jesus used when he founded his "church" gave them a different picture from the one you and I have today.

While the language He used was crystal clear to them, much of it is (literally) lost in translation for us. What did Jesus intend the church to be? The truth is he really did not even say he was going to build a "church." So what did Jesus intend the church to be? Let's look at what He said to Peter.

> *When Jesus came to the region of Caesarea Philippi, he asked his disciples, "Who do people say the Son of Man is?" They replied, "Some say John the Baptist; others say Elijah; and still others, Jeremiah or one of the prophets." "But what about you?" he asked. "Who do you say I am?" Simon Peter answered, "You are the Messiah, the Son of the living God." Jesus replied, "Blessed are you, Simon son of Jonah, for this was not revealed to you by flesh and blood, but by my Father in heaven. And I tell you that you are Peter, and on this rock I will build my **church**, and the gates of Hades will not overcome it. (Matthew 16:13-18 NIV)*

Peter is blessed because He has been given a revelation from God. And that revelation–that Jesus is the Messiah–will be the cornerstone of what He is about to build, His church. Yet if we look a little more closely at this scripture, we find that Jesus really didn't tell Peter He was going to build a church. He was going to build something else. But what?

The word "church" isn't the right word to translate from the original language in this verse. If we trace the word church through its history, we see that it comes from the old English and German word, *kirche*. This German word traces back to the Greek word *kuriakos* (Strong's 2960).

The root of *kuriakos* is *kurios*, meaning "lord." It also carries the meaning of that which "pertains to" or "belongs to a lord." We see it used in 1 Corinthians 11:20 as Paul talks about the proper procedures for the Lord's Supper and again in Revelation 1:10 when John was in the Spirit on the Lord's Day.

This word and its variations are used over 700 times in the New Testament. Each time this Greek word is used, it is translated with the connotation of a "lord" or a "master." The word "church" is actually an accurate translation of the Greek word *kuriakon*.

If Jesus had said in Matthew 16, "Upon this rock I will build my *kuriakon*," it would also have been correct to use the word "church" to translate it. This, however, isn't the word found in the Greek; instead, it's the word *ekklésia* (Strong's 1577).

Jesus was not planning to build a building. He was coming to call people out of the world's system and into his own.

The Ekklésia

It is important to distinguish the connotations of *ekklésia* from *kuriakos* so we know what Jesus had in his mind. The *kuriakos* was that which belonged to a lord. In truth, we do belong to the Lord. While we do belong to the Lord and are his possession, the word *ekklésia* carries with it a much deeper meaning, purpose, and mission.

The word *ekklésia* comes from *ek* (Strong's 1537), "out from," and *kaleó* (Strong's 2564), "to call"; therefore, the Greek word *ekklésia* is literally translated as "the called-out ones." It denotes a people, a purpose, an assembly or congregation, a group convened for a particular purpose. Jesus was building a group of "called-out ones." But called out to what?

In Greece the *ekklésia* was the "gathering of those summoned." They were the group called out to govern, make policy, and rule.[3] It was the governing body of the city of Athens. Every male citizen above the age of 20 was entitled to join this assembly. They met to discuss matters of state and commerce. They were the ruling body. They passed laws, governed, and brought order to society.[4] Jesus' disciples understood He was going to establish a group of people to govern and rule.

The disciples also understood the word *ekklésia* as a translation of a Hebrew word with which they were familiar. In the Septuagint (the Greek translation of the Hebrew Old Testament), the

Greek word *ekklésia* is used to translate the Hebrew word *qahal*. This word described the nation of Israel, called out as God's special people. Jesus was saying He was establishing a nation.

The word *qahal* was also used for meetings of the leaders of Israel called together for the purpose of preparing war plans or conducting civil affairs and bears the same meaning as the contemporary view of the word as used for the assembly of Athens, called to govern. [5]

So while a church typically brings images of a building, the *ekklésia* carries with it the connotation of a movement, a cause, a call, and a group of people called out of the world's system to be the new government of Christ established in the hearts of men. *Ekklésia* speaks specifically of the people Jesus will call out of every other religious order to himself.

The Church Is God's Kingdom

Jesus was not planning to build a building. He was coming to call people out of the world's system and into his own. He was beginning a revolution. Jesus was establishing His Kingdom. His disciples thought it was a political and earthly one. They assumed He was preparing to overthrow the Roman government and re-establish the kingdom of Israel. They mistook His intentions all the way to the ascension in the book of Acts:

> *Then they gathered around him and asked him, "Lord, are you at this time going to restore the kingdom to Israel?" (Acts 1:6 NIV)*

We look back at the disciples and wonder how they failed to understand that Jesus was not going to establish a physical throne in Jerusalem and set up His new government. Yet the language Jesus used to describe the "church" was not a building but a government, a kingdom.

The early church was not a group of sitting saints; it was a group of summoned soldiers.

King of Hearts

It wasn't until the Holy Spirit came that they fully began to understand they already *were* the Kingdom. They had been established as the *ekklésia*, called out of the world's system to fulfill the mission of Jesus. They were to establish a kingdom in the hearts of men–one without borders, one without ethnic barriers, and one that permitted citizenship to Jew and Gentile alike.

They knew that when Jesus said he would build his *ekklésia*, he was not speaking of brick and mortar. He was speaking of assembling a band of people that would have only one agenda: Advance the Kingdom. They would have no other desires, loyalties, or allegiances. They would follow the one and only King, Jesus. Their fervor was so strong that the book of Acts records the charges made regarding their disloyalty to the government:

> *They are all defying Caesar's decrees, saying that there is another king, one called Jesus. (Acts 17:7 NIV)*

While most of the modern day church is afraid of Hell, Hell was afraid of the *ekklésia*. It was a revolution that would change the world. Their movement was so powerful the gates (the governments) of Hell could not withstand their advancing march.

They did not spend their time fretting over the news or wringing their hands over the latest stock market report. They did not pin their hopes on who controlled the government at the time or who was up for re-election. They were forming a different government. They were fully committed to one agenda in the world: "Your kingdom come, Your will be done, on Earth as it is in Heaven."

This powerful organism that Jesus left here on Earth was so pure and so radical that it turned the world upside down! They began a revolution using only spiritual swords and the power of the Holy Spirit acting upon the hearts of men. They intended to overthrow the kingdom of darkness and bring men into the kingdom of God, and they did. Under tremendous pressure, with threat of beatings, and through imprisonments and pain of death they devoted themselves to advancing the cause of Christ. They endured these hardships as soldiers fighting a noble battle. In all their painful circumstances, they continued unphased and unstoppable. They were not sitting saints, they were summoned soldiers. They did not *go* to church; they *were* the church. Their concern was not erecting edifices but ending evil–establishing Christ's government in the hearts of men.

Sid Roth says of the early church leaders, "[They] weren't 'church builders' in the sense that we may have thought of them. They weren't advocating people now find some place where they can be separate and not influence anyone around them, meeting for a few hours on the weekend and singing a few songs, hearing a message, and then going home. These men were Kingdom builders! They were dethroning Caesar and the whole Roman governmental structure with its Empire class structure in the minds of the people."[6]

So why has the modern church in the United States lost so much of this power? Where did we get the idea that the church was a place instead of a people? When did we stop being the *ekklésia* and start going to *kuriakos*? When we say "church," why do we think "building"? To answer that we will take a look at our spiritual history.

Old Pattern

The Old Testament pattern of interaction with God was centered around Holy Places and the House of God. After an encounter with God, His people often built monuments and altars to commemorate the experience. They respected and remembered places as sacred or holy.

Moses received a plan from God to construct a tent of meeting, a house in which God's very presence would dwell among his people. This portable house gave God a means of being near His people. He traveled ahead of the Children of Israel until they camped and set up the tabernacle again where God would re-enter and remain in His house. To be near God and worship Him the people would go to the tabernacle.

When David became king, it occurred to him that while he

lived in a nice house, God still dwelled in a tent. He desired to build a permanent house for God to honor Him; however, David's son Solomon would be the one to do it. David commissioned Solomon to complete the temple when he had taken the throne.

> *Then Solomon began to build the temple of the Lord in Jerusalem on Mount Moriah, where the Lord had appeared to his father David. It was on the threshing floor of Araunah the Jebusite, the place provided by David. (2 Chronicles 3:1 NIV)*

While the tabernacle had been temporary, the temple gave God a permanent house among his people. The pattern of going to the House of the Lord to worship God continued.

This first edition of the temple was destroyed by Nebuchadnezzar II in 586 B.C. Israel's place of worship, the house for God's presence, was destroyed. The people of Israel longed for God's house to be reconstructed so they could resume their worship of God and have His presence again in His house.

The temple was rebuilt with construction completed in 515 B.C. God's house had been rebuilt. Israel once again had a place to go to worship.

New Pattern

This second edition of the temple was the one in Jerusalem where Jesus conducted his earthly ministry. In a prophetic utterance, Jesus foretells the destruction of the temple:

"Do you see all these things?" he asked. "Truly I tell you, not one stone here will be left on another; every one will be thrown down." (Matthew 24:2 NIV)

This prophecy directly outlines how the temple will be destroyed a second time. For those who were following the teachings of Jesus, this must have been a terrible prediction to hear. They had lost it once before, and now Jesus predicts it will happen again.

Yet Jesus went beyond prophesying that the temple would be destroyed. He spoke of a time in which a building would no longer be needed for His followers to worship Him. This prediction took place when Jesus was speaking with the woman at the well. She asked him to settle a dispute about the proper place for people to go to worship. The answer Jesus gave predicted the future pattern of worship the *ekklésia* would follow to worship Him.

*"Sir," the woman said, "you must be a prophet. So tell me, why is it that you Jews insist that Jerusalem is the only place of worship, while we Samaritans claim it is here at Mount Gerizim, where our ancestors worshiped?" Jesus replied, "Believe me, dear woman, the time is coming when **it will no longer matter whether you worship the Father on this mountain or in Jerusalem.**" (John 4:19-21 NLT)*

You cannot *go* to the House of the Lord.
You *are* the House of the Lord.

The Samaritan woman received a sneak peak of how things would be done in the new order He was about to establish. Jesus said worship would not be centered around structures, but the spirit. His worshippers would no longer be confined to a building. His sacrifice would do away with the necessity of temple sacrifice and worship. Though it would be years before the Temple was physically destroyed, Jesus knew that from the moment of His death it would no longer be necessary. To emphasize this change, the veil in the temple was torn in two upon His death.

> *"At that moment the curtain in the sanctuary of the Temple was torn in two, from top to bottom. (Matthew 27:51 NLT)*

This event symbolized that the physical temple was empty and no longer needed. God would no longer dwell in a temple made with human hands. He was relocating!

Paul told us where the new temple is: "Don't you realize that your body is the **temple** of the Holy Spirit, who lives in you and was given to you by God?" (1 Corinthians 6:19 NLT)

The word temple is the Greek word *naos* (Strong's #3485). It refers to the Most Holy Place. This was the place in the tabernacle and the temple where the presence of God resided. In other words, Paul said you and I have become the dwelling place of God. *We* are the house of God. *We* are the sanctuary. *We* are the temple. Wherever we are, there God is. We carry his presence with us. While the Old Testament pattern was centered around Holy Places and the

House of God, the New Testament pattern is Holy People who *are* the House of God.

You cannot *go* to the House of the Lord. You *are* the house of the Lord. We do not go to visit him on the weekend. He is always with us. Wherever we go, God goes also because His dwelling is in us. We do not leave God in the building when we exit the building. You cannot *go* to church, because you *are* the church. This is not simply semantics. The language is subtle, but the implications are substantial.

The early church was not a group of part-time believers who showed up on Sunday to hear a sermon and then return to their normal lives.

We say well-meaning things without realizing their implications. For instance, if we say "It's good to be in the House of the Lord, today," it implies we have had an out-of-body experience all week. We cannot simply enter and exit the house of the Lord at will because our body *is* the house of the Lord. To use this phrase correctly at a worship service, we should say, "Welcome, houses of the Lord, to our worship service today."

Further, many of us call the place we gather to worship "the sanctuary." While that may be true in one sense–that we gather there and find rest and refreshing, it is not true in the sense that it is the dwelling place of God. The place we gather to worship is not the sanctuary. We are. Instead of traveling to a temple, tabernacle, sanctuary, or house of God, we carry Him with us. We are a walking, moving place where God is manifested.

The Power of the New

The disciples understood the emphasis changed from a place to a **people**! They were the new temple–the sanctuary–and were called to be the *ekklésia*–a body of people called out for a cause. With this understanding they knew they were carriers of God's presence 24 hours per day, 7 days per week, 365 days per year.

The early church was not a group of part-time believers who showed up on Sunday to hear a sermon and then return to their normal lives. Ministry was not confined to the temple, but it took to the streets. "Churches" were not rated by the volume of the music or the length of the sermons but on the encounter between God and man, wherever that might happen to be. The believers were on a full-time mission: to be the *ekklésia*. They believed what Jesus said. They could not go to church; they were the church. Because they believed this concept so deeply, the church expanded rapidly despite substantial opposition.

The Pull of the Old

Persecution was a threat to the church throughout its early history. Christians were seen as threats to the established form of worship at the time. Depending on the fervor of the governing leaders at the time, Christians might be imprisoned or martyred. In 313 A.D. Emperor Constantine did the unimaginable. He issued the Edict of Milan decriminalizing Christian worship.

Imagine the sigh of relief of Christians across the country. There must have been countless celebrations of joy, gratitude, and thankfulness to God for finally answering prayers and cries for relief. While it was certainly a time for celebration, what was to come of the church would be something other than what Jesus left as the *ekklésia*. The landscape of Christianity would be forever changed. In 380 A.D. Nicene Christianity became the state church of the Roman Empire.

What had, until this point, been a group of people wholly dedicated to the mission of Christ in the world was now in the hands of the government. Church and state were synonymous. Constantine gave Christians a new temple called "church" (*kuriakos*), also known as "The House of the Lord." Christians would cease to be the *ekklésia*; they would go to a *kuriakos*.

When the church came to mean a building, it was somewhere to *go*, not someone to *be*. Remember the exercise from earlier in which you described the location of your church? Odds are it was not even second nature to begin thinking of the building, the place where the church gathers. Still today, we have lost much of the meaning of the *ekklésia* and have settled for attending a *kuriakos*.

**Jesus did not come to build a building
but to start a revolution.**

I believe this explains much of why we find the church weak and ineffective today. There are few connections to our daily life. Few of us understand what it really means to be a disciple, an ambassador, a solider, or part of the *ekklésia*. Without the need to be constantly ready for action, many Christians do not pray, read their

Bible, share their faith, or serve their local congregation. There are few connections between "church" and "real life." We no longer consider ourselves as a missional movement. The name Christian simply means "I'm not Muslim, Buddhist, or Hindu."

Today most people are content to go to a building that is made of brick and mortar–their "church." They go through the motions to sing a few songs, listen to a message, give their offerings, and go home. Now finished with their religious requirements for the week, they can go back to their secular jobs, secular homes, and secular lives. People are content to go to the building rather than to be the church.

We must remind ourselves of the original intention of Jesus when He said He would build His Church. If we think He intended to construct buildings, we will be forever working diligently yet in the wrong direction. Jesus did not come to build a building but to start a revolution.

A New Beginning

The nature of the *ekklésia* is a foundational concept for Second Mile Leadership. Just as the early church understood, we must reclaim the meaning of being the *ekklésia*, 24 hours per day, 7 days per week, 365 days per year. When we fully grasp this idea, we, too, will be unstoppable.

What if we fully understood that we are a missional band of God's people with no ruler or government besides God? What might happen if we had no other real agenda in the world other than expanding the Kingdom of God? What if we were always looking for opportunities to bring divine presence to daily life? What if we realized that every person is a minister and should be in the process of being equipped for ministry rather than receiving it? What if we were soldiers looking for a fight instead of sheep longing to be fed?

> *The church, you see, is not peripheral to the world; the world is peripheral to the church.*
> *(Ephesians 1:23 MSG)*

The Bible tells us that the church should be the center of our worlds, not a sidenote. So if you believed you were called to be part of a group of people with no loyalty to any earthly agenda other than expanding God's kingdom on earth, what would you change? What would you do on your job? What would you do in the marketplace? How would you spend your time? How would you spend your money?

If a group of people under severe persecution could advance the gospel and expand the kingdom of God under those circumstances, what is our excuse? We have every available resource at our fingertips and live in a free nation.

The truth is that if God were done with the church influencing the world He would take us home to Heaven, but there are still people to be saved and to come into the family of God. The church has to remember what it is supposed to be and become it once more!

I am calling you back to the original intention of Jesus–that he could build his *ekklésia* and all the governments of Hell could not stop it. It is time to return to the purpose and the plan of God in your life.

We need to become discontent with going to a *kuriakos* and start being the *ekklésia*. We have been spectators long enough. We have been distracted by the desires of the world long enough. We have been blinded to God's purpose in our lives long enough. It is time to become the *ekklésia*.

IT'S TIME TO STOP **GOING** TO CHURCH AND START **BEING** THE CHURCH!

2

IT'S NOT ABOUT ME

I like your Christ; I do not like your Christians.
Your Christians are so unlike your Christ.
- Gandhi

When Aimee and I were first married, I was a waiter at a Chinese restaurant. Thankfully our living expenses were minimal, the restaurant was popular, and I was a fairly good waiter. I worked quickly and efficiently, doing my best to make sure that people had their food in a timely manner and presented to their specifications. To my recollection, I only had one incident in which I dumped some tea into a customer's lap–a pretty good track record if you ask me. The owner of the restaurant was a nice Chinese lady, and in her accent would often call me a "soop-uh wait-uh" (super waiter). This was a great compliment, sometimes offset by her threats to "quit you" (fire me). It was a great job, and I gained valuable experience in customer service.

From time to time I would be fortunate enough to get one of "those" customers. One that, no matter how hard I tried, I simply could not please. Their food was undercooked. Then it was overcooked. It was too cold. It was too hot. My service was too fast. My service was too slow. Their tea glass had been empty for more than two minutes, or I should not have filled their glass. To their dismay and disdain, I had destroyed their delicate balance of tea-to-sugar ratio.

Having worked in a restaurant, I get very nervous when I go out to eat with friends who complain and are rude to the waitstaff. When they demand their food make a second trip to and from the kitchen, I shudder. I can only imagine what extra "ingredients" may be added to their dish on its second trip from the kitchen to the table. Based on my experience in the industry, my advice is to be kind to your waiters and waitresses when there are problems with your meal.

The restaurant I worked at had one of "those" customers as a frequent offender. He found something wrong with our service or food no matter how hard we worked to satisfy his demands. One of his primary complaints was that his food was never spicy enough. Each time he ordered we would increase the crushed-red-pepper-and-oil substance (laja) in an effort to please him. No matter how much we added, we could never get it hot enough.

After one of his visits, we decided that the next time he came we would spice his food to the level no human should be able to tolerate. When he was seated, we informed our head cook that he was back. "Wong," we said, "that guy who complains his food is never spicy enough is back." We watched as Wong filled an *entire ladle* with the pepper and oil and *covered* the guy's plate. His meal was mostly pepper and oil with a side of food. We were convinced this would be the time the guy either confessed it was hot enough or he would stop eating at our restaurant.

Can you guess what he said? You are right. It was not hot enough. As this customer sat eating his food, his face was leaking from every orifice; yet he still claimed it was not spicy. We were dumbfounded and exasperated. At this point, we realized we would never be able to meet his standard or demands. If we met his expectations, he would simply move the bar.

That man was a lot like many of us today. We cannot be satisfied. Maybe this is because we live in a culture that tells us we should not be. We are told that everything in our world revolves around us.

The I's Have It

In the United States we have crowned the individual king! Marketing strategies, moms, and dads have raised a generation to believe they are the center of the universe. Life revolves around them. Their desires matter more than than anyone else's. They believe they are endowed with more than the right to *pursue* happiness; they believe they are entitled to it. Our new cultural norms reinforce the idea that the individual is the most important person in the world.

Advances in technology have placed communication, entertainment, and media in the palm of our hands. Each person is now able to have his own individual music and media consumption devices. Our cars, once a bastion of noise of arguments, fussing, and fighting are now eerily silent as each person throws in his earbuds, tunes in to his own world, and tunes out everyone else. We no longer complain about what station we listen to on the radio in the car because it is never on. We can choose whatever we want with our phones, tablets, or mp3 players. Zoned out in our own personal space, "Are we there yet?" is replaced with "Oh, Wow! We are there?"

Cooperation and consideration are relics of antiquity. Now each of us can choose what he wants, when he wants. Unlimited TV streaming allows each family member to watch his own shows that meet his own tastes in his own room. Expensive television systems are no longer needed. Each person has a personal TV in his hand. The brand names of many of these devices are aptly named with the first letter being "i." The person in control is the "i." I am able to watch what I want, when I want, where I want.

The individual not only has entertainment at his fingertips but also the best the marketplace has to offer as well. The competition of capitalism drives retailers to produce the best quality at the lowest price. Mass production of technology and textiles allows the individual consumer access to goods and services that are far out of reach for most of the world. Our marketing and distribution system allows items to be produced and sold so inexpensively that we consider many of them disposable. Products that would have required second mortgages in years past are so affordable today that we simply discard them when the new model arrives on the market. If we purchase an item and later decide we do not like it, we might not even bother to return it. The hassle of the return is too great.

As the consumer, we expect competition to give us the best for the least. If a store fails to stock our desired item or sells it at a higher price than its competitor, down the street we go. Our loyalty is to whoever is able to satisfy our demands and cater to us as the customer.

It may sound as if I am not in favor of capitalism and competition. That is not true. I am thankful I live in a nation that has free markets. Capitalism, consumerism, and mass distribution of products are largely responsible for our ability to live with the quality of life we enjoy. What was unattainable for previous generations is status quo for many people who live in the United States today. Almost everyone today is able to live at a standard beyond the kings of yesterday.

While abuse is in the system, free market competition is a good thing. We would never be able to afford the luxuries we have without this system in place. Today we carry more computing power in our pockets than we previously were able to fit into a large room. How free markets, competition, and consumerism have driven us to produce such incredible products and inventions is astounding.

As with any new thing, our appreciation diminishes over time. What caused us to be overwhelmed with gratitude yesterday, we take for granted today. To have blessing of this magnitude so readily available to us moves us from appreciation to expectation. We forget just how fast and how far we have come to this new place of abundance.

In this new normal, we are conditioned to consumer convenience. The marketplace caters to us. As the customer, we are always right. Sales people woo us with offers. Managers make great efforts to please us and retain our business.

This is the expectation and the standard in the marketplace. When we bring this philosophy into the church and expect it to operate the same way, however, the consequences are devastating!

**We have turned the church into a corporation
and become its fickle customers.**

Consumer Christians

If we bring the consumer mind-set into the church, it produces certain behaviors that may seem normal but do not belong. We choose churches based on what they have to offer. We stay as long as they cater to us. We attend as long as we like the music, temperature, messages, people, parking, presentation, and expectations. When our preferences are not met or our comfort is challenged, we leave. After all, we are the customer, and the customer is always right. Right?

We treat the church just as any other company or corporation. We expect it to anticipate and meet our needs. We assume that, as any good company would, it will conduct market research to allow us to contribute our opinion. When we have weighed in with our feedback and ratings, we expect church management to tweak the environment and experience so we'll feel good vibes and want to return next week. If the church is expert at meeting our desires, needs, and wishes, we will be loyal–as long as they have close parking, Disney-like children's experiences, no request for us to serve, or God forbid! an appeal to *give*.

When our expectations are not met, we simply eject from one congregation and try the next one down the street. Whether or not we verbalize it, our thoughts are "Haven't you heard? It's all about me."

If we are ever to be effective as the *Ekklésia* , we have to understand and embrace this idea: It's not about me.

We come by this behavior naturally as citizens in the United States. This has been ingrained in us through marketing for years. It is our mantra. Because we see the church as just another corporation, we bring that same consumer mind-set along with us. We superimpose that mind-set on the church.

We've forgotten that we are the *ekklésia*–the called-*out* ones. We are called *out* from culture. Called *out* to live differently. Called *out* to be ambassadors of the kingdom in which we find our citizenship, which incidentally is not the U.S.A. Called *out* to represent the interests and enterprise of the kingdom of Heaven.

We have turned the church into a corporation and become its fickle customers. We have exchanged contributing for consuming. We have made the church about "me."

Should it really come as a surprise when parents expect to leave their children in fully staffed, immaculate nurseries while refusing to serve on the team or give a dime to the church? Should worship teams be shocked when people are not impressed with their music? Should pastors expect mass movements of people to change upon hearing the Word? Certainly not when the mind-set of people attending is "It's all about me." While consumer Christians attend, ready to rate the church based on their experience, exhausted leaders scream the famous line of the movie, *The Gladiator,* "***Are you not entertained***?!"

It's Not About Me

The idea that the church is all about me flies in the face of what Jesus taught and showed us. When it comes to the kingdom of God, we know that it *includes* me, but it's not *about* me. If we are ever to be effective as the *ekklésia*, we have to understand and embrace this idea: **It's not about me**.

Jesus never called the individual to elevate himself; instead, He called us to humble ourselves. He taught us to take the lowest seat at the table. He said the greatest would be the servant of all. He said the first shall be last and the last shall be first. He modeled this for us. Philippians says that we should act like Jesus.

> *You must have the same attitude that Christ Jesus had. Though he was God, he did not think of equality with God as something to cling to. Instead, he gave up his divine privileges; he took the humble position of a slave. (Philippians 2:5-7 NLT)*

If ever anyone could have rightfully uttered the phrase, "It's about me," it would have been Jesus. It *was* and *is* about Him. He had divine rights, and He had privileges, but He gave them up. He humbled Himself and took up the position of a slave. If our *Savior* did this, shouldn't we?

We know this is exactly what we should do, but it runs countercultural to the philosophy we've been taught. We have been told we should elevate ourselves. We should seek our own way. Burger King even tells us we can "Have it your way!"

Unfortunately many Christians bring these ideas and this philosophy into the church. Ask the pastor of your church how many times he gets complaints about what people don't like. Let him tell you the stories of people making demands for change to accommodate their personal preferences. Ask him if anyone has ever threatened to move his membership and money to the church down the street if things didn't go his way.

The mission is more important than my personal preferences.

You may be surprised to learn that some of these things happen. It should not, but it does. When people expect the church to run like an American company, they cannot help but consider the various churches as a marketplace to cater to their needs just as a variety of grocery stores. There are plenty of churches to choose from. They keep shopping until they find one that will cater to their preferences.

The Mission Is More Than Me

Jesus did not espouse this philosophy or model this behavior. He instead made the mission more important than His own desires, preferences, and wishes. He modeled a life that valued mission over self-interest.

He showed us in the Garden of Gethsemane just how much

bigger the mission of God is in the world. In that place his soul went through torture as He faced the reality of the physical, emotional, and spiritual pain He was about to endure on our behalf. He wrestled so hard against His will and emotions that the capillaries in His skin burst and He literally began to sweat blood.

Matthew tells us, "He fell with his face to the ground and prayed, 'My Father, if it is possible, may this cup be taken from Me.'" Jesus was asking the Father, "Can You find another way? Can You see a different course? I really don't want to do this."

Notice Jesus closely, however. He finishes, "Yet not as I will, but as You will." (Matthew 26:39) Wow. Our God and Savior, Jesus Christ, accepted the worst possible path to complete the mission. In that garden, He begged God for another way and then chose death on the cross because there was not one.

God's dream is bigger than our our desires. The call is greater than our comfort. The mission is more than me.

In the account of His prayer in the garden, Jesus showed us there is something more important that the individual–the mission. It's more important than I am. It's more important than my preferences. It's more important than my desires.

One of my huge frustrations is having people in the church tell me they cannot serve in an area because they aren't "gifted" or "passionate" about that ministry. They tell me they just aren't "fulfilled" there. I do believe God uniquely and specifically shapes us so that we are fitted to his specific calling in our lives. We do our best to discover the design God placed in each person and release each to serve there. If, however, we can't be asked to mop a floor or serve in a nursery because it's outside what our spiritual gifts assessment and passion profile show for us, I say we have missed the point altogether.

The mission is more important than my personal preferences. To walk away from that need because it's not "my" thing is to say the mission isn't important to me. That does not resemble the kind of life Christ lived or the one He calls us to. Jesus modeled this idea for us. The mission is greater than me.

Because we have settled for a me-centered gospel, we have lost the meaning of the word "Christian."

Deep down we know this. We long to live for something greater than ourselves. This is why men cry as they see images of heroism of men giving their lives to save others. We know that there is no more noble thing we can do than to give our lives so others can keep theirs. Jesus told us there is no greater love than this. (John 15:13)

Somehow we've lost the idea that the mission of Christ is the all-important purpose of our lives–all of ours. It is not just the mission of the pastor or the staff of the church, but all of us who call ourselves "Christians" or "disciples." God's dream is bigger than our our desires. The call is greater than our comfort. The mission is more than me.

Christian or Disciple?

Then he said to the crowd, "If any of you wants to be my
follower, you must turn from your selfish ways, take up
your cross daily, and follow me. If you try to hang on to
your life, you will lose it. But if you give up your life for
my sake, you will save it. And what do you benefit if you
gain the whole world but are yourself lost or destroyed?
(Luke 9:23-35 NLT)

David Platt, in his book *Radical*, says it like this: "I ... think that somewhere along the way we ... missed what is radical about our faith and replaced it with what is comfortable. We [are] settling for a Christianity that revolves around catering to ourselves when the central message of Christianity is actually about abandoning ourselves."[7]

Just like the word "church", the word "Christian" has become fairly ambiguous. The name carries a range of connotations, from being a fully obedient follower of Christ to simply being more associated with the Christian religious persuasion than other religions. Because we have settled for a me-centered gospel, we have lost the meaning of the word "Christian."

Jesus used a different word for this followers. He called them "disciples." There is no ambiguity in that word. To be a disciple means you learn and *obey* the teachings of your master. Many Christians give themselves the option of obeying or neglecting the commands of Jesus. Disciples do not have this option. Obedience is the only way.

As Jesus comes to the conclusion of His earthly ministry, He gives His final command to His disciples. In Matthew 28, He tells his disciples what he is leaving them to do: to carry out the mission that He started. The rest of their lives would be spent living out this mission because they were His disciples.

He further told these disciples to "make disciples." He told them to "teach these new disciples to obey everything I have commanded you." (Matthew 28:20) Obeying all the commands of Christ means the new disciples were also called to make disciples. There is a continuation and perpetuation of the purpose that was on the *original* disciples. While a Christian may be someone associated with Christ, a disciple *obeys* Him.

So, are you a disciple or a Christian? A disciple carries that original purpose Jesus gave in Matthew 28–to make more disciples. Disciples realize that they are in this world for God's purpose and not their own. If throughout our lives we consume our time, energy, and resources on us, the Bible is very clear that we will give an account of what we have done with what we have been given. It should be about His mission. It's not about me.

Jesus demands extreme commitment of His disciples. In Luke chapter 9, three men have an encounter with Jesus and an opportunity to become His disciples.

> *As they were walking along, someone said to Jesus, "I will follow you wherever you go." But Jesus replied, "Foxes have dens to live in, and birds have nests, but the Son*

of Man has no place even to lay his head." (Luke 9: 57-58 NLT)

This man voluntarily chooses Jesus. He was not compelled by a pastor to come forward to an altar. He simply responded to his heart's cry to follow Christ. He makes a bold commitment to follow Jesus, wherever that leads.

The purpose of God may call us from the family with which we share blood and to the family with which we share mission.

Jesus responds in a way that would confuse most church leaders today. He essentially discourages this man by informing him that He does not know where He is going. He will go wherever the mission dictates. He lets him know that foxes and birds always know where they are going to lay their heads down at night–home. The animals are able to go back to the comfortable and familiar–what they have always known. Jesus is informing the man that following Him does not offer this same guarantee. Jesus tells him essentially, " If you want to follow me, you might just find yourself homeless."

In the second encounter, Jesus calls a man to discipleship. He offers the invitation to enter a disciple relationship:

He said to another person, "Come, follow me." The man agreed, but he said, "Lord, first let me return home and bury my father." But Jesus told him, "Let the

spiritually dead bury their own dead! Your duty is to go
and preach about the Kingdom of God." (Luke 9:59-60
NLT)

Jesus informs the second man that the cost of following him might be the luxury of permanence in family. It might mean we aren't able to be near our "blood" family in their critical moments or special days. In another passage, Jesus tells who His family really is—those who do the will of the Father. The purpose of God may call us from the family with which we share blood and to the family with which we share mission. Holidays dinners may look a little different for those who say yes to being a disciple.

At first glance, Jesus honestly comes off as very calloused and rude. He seems to lack compassion. It appears He does not care about this man's situation, but the reality is that He sees from an eternal perspective, not just our temporal viewpoint. The mission is sometimes more important than mourning. We see this in the life of Jesus immediately after He hears the news of the death of John the Baptist. He wants to have some "me time" to be alone. Matthew tells us what happened:

As soon as Jesus heard the news, he left in a boat to a
remote area to be alone. But the crowds heard where he
was headed and followed on foot from many towns. Je-
sus saw the huge crowd as he stepped from the boat, and
he had compassion on them and healed their sick.
(Matthew 14:13-14 NLT)

While I have seen people rise to this level of commitment, I have to ask myself, "Is my commitment to the call at this level?" Would I suppress my emotions and ignore my own need in a time such as this to do ministry like Jesus did?

Several years ago at one of our Saturday night services, my Pastor, Steve Pyle, was getting ready to preach the message. Just before he stepped onto the stage, he received word that his uncle and aunt were in a motorcycle accident on their way to the church. We knew the accident was bad, but details were still emerging. Ambulances were on the scene. The situation did not look good for either of them. We would learn later that the aunt died at the scene of the accident and the uncle was critically injured.

While several of the family broke down in agonizing cries within earshot of the auditorium, Pastor Steve kept his composure. While the remainder of his family rushed to the hospital, he preached the message and made a call for people to follow Christ. Only when the service was over did he go to the hospital.

While he would have loved to be able to go immediately, the mission was more important in that moment. He had a duty to fulfill. From our natural perspective, it might have seemed like an indifferent attitude on his part. Although his aunt had stepped into eternity, she had done so ready to meet Jesus. His uncle was in critical condition, but he also was ready to meet the Lord.

Pastor Steve knew the people sitting in the pews of the auditorium had the same eternal destiny, but many of them were not ready for the appointment. In that moment the mission was more important than his emotion. Helping others prepare to meet Christ was the most important decision to be made. Once those preparations were made, he was free to go and be with the family.

The third interaction of Luke 9 goes as follows:

Another said, "Yes, Lord, I will follow you, but first let me say goodbye to my family." But Jesus told him, "Anyone who puts a hand to the plow and then looks back is not fit for the Kingdom of God." (Luke 9:61-62 NLT)

Jesus was saying, "The mission is ahead of you, not behind you. If you're going to follow me, now is your chance. I demand absolute commitment to the mission. Are you ready to leave home without saying goodbye?"

Sometimes the call of God takes us from family, friends, and the familiar. This may involve relocation from family or the place we have always called home. He may call us to adopt a new people or group just as Ruth did with Naomi. If we are going to be a part of the *ekklésia*, we have to put our hand to the task of the mission and look forward, not backward.

Many of us want the benefit of Christ without the sacrifice. Yet Christ may call us to the sacrifice without the benefit.

As far as we can tell from this passage, Jesus talked these guys out of following Him. We really do not know what they did. In an examination of my own life and desires, I shudder to think what choice I would have made in this moment. I wonder if I would have missed my moment to walk with the Messiah.

I think this gives us an opportunity for personal reflection. Are we ready to answer the call to be more than a Christian? Are we ready to become a disciple, or have we swallowed the lie of culture that it's all about me? Why have we chosen to follow Christ? Is our commitment more than just a fire escape? Many of us want the benefit of Christ without the sacrifice. Yet Christ may call us to the sacrifice without the benefit.

David Platt says, "Jesus [called his disciples] to abandon themselves. They were leaving certainty for uncertainty, safety for danger. In a world that prizes promoting oneself, they were following a teacher who told them to crucify themselves. And history tells us the result. Almost all of them would lose their lives because they responded to his invitation."[8]

To accept Christ means to adopt his mission. Jesus calls us to choose His cause and to surrender our own! If we are to be Second Mile Leaders, we have to understand that He is calling us into a mission that is bigger than a single individual. It's not about me!

It's Me Again

The pull of our flesh and culture is to keep turning the mission inward and making it about me again and again. The good news is we are not alone in our selfishness. We are not the only ones to get it wrong. We have good company with the 12 men that Jesus called to be his disciples.

In Mark 10, James and John come and ask Jesus if they can get reserved seats on his left and right when he sets up His Kingdom.

He tells them their desires to be first are going to place them dead last. He tells them promotion in His Kingdom looks like demotion everywhere else. He wants them to stop making everything about them. He says, *"Even the Son of Man came not to be served but to serve others and give his life as a ransom for many." (Mark 10:45 NLT)*

When He uses the phrase "even the Son of Man," Jesus is saying if anyone has the right to exaltation, glory, and the throne it is He. He is not elevating himself now, however; He is taking on the position of a servant in order to fulfill the mission.

How does this play out in your life and mine? We are to be about the same mission Jesus was—to seek and save the lost. Our job is to bring people out of the kingdom of darkness and into the *ekklésia*, God's kingdom, His Church.

As the Church, we exist for those who are unsaved. As a Second Mile Leader, we are to create environments and encounters between those outside the Kingdom and Jesus. Just like Jesus, we are not here to *be* served. We are here *to* serve.

Is your weekend attendance at church all about being served, getting your needs met, getting what you want, your way? Then maybe you have not become a disciple. Perhaps you are an interested investigator or a curious observer, but not a disciple.

If you're going to be a Second Mile Leader, you have to stop looking at what the church can do to benefit you and start looking for what you can do to benefit the church!

My goal as a pastor is to make sure that every team member is in service as much as possible. I am also looking, however, for them to be willing to give up their seat, worship experience, message time, parking space, and anything else we so frequently label "mine" in order to serve the mission.

Instead of diverting resources toward you by whining and complaining, why not become a resource to new people to help meet their needs and connect with them? Instead of pointing out problems, why not provide solutions? Instead of proudly serving only where it fits your preferences, why not humbly offer to serve in the areas of greatest need? That's what Jesus did, and that's what Second Mile Leaders do.

When it comes to the weekend service at church, you should have this attitude: I am not here for me; I am here to serve. If I am able to be served, that is great! If, however, I am unable to sit down, that is also fine. My main mission is to help others meet Jesus. I'm not here to participate; I'm here to facilitate. I'm not going to sit; I'm going to serve. This is why Second Mile Leaders excel at exceeding expectations.

Most people come to service looking to be fed. Second Mile Leaders come ready to distribute the food they've received in personal devotion during the week. Most people come to receive prayer. Second Mile Leaders come ready to pray for others. Regular attenders come ready for "my worship time." Second Mile Leaders worship all seven days a week, so if they miss corporate worship occasionally they are just fine. Consumers say, "I'll serve where I'm gifted." Second Mile Leaders serve wherever there is a need.

Second Mile Leaders make it easy for new people by parking farther away. They serve on the welcome team, making people immediately feel loved and welcome. They walk them through the building, showing them where to find the things they need. They walk people to and from their cars with umbrellas when it rains.

As a disciple who makes disciples, a Second Mile Leader has these thoughts: I am *responsible* for others. My time on the weekend and throughout the week should be to help others learn and obey Jesus' commands. I am here to make disciples.

Killing The Me Monster

To be a Second Mile Leader we must must unlearn the American way. We need a divorce from the "me first" idea. We require deliverance from the "I" of idolatry. We have to adopt this philosophy: It's not about me.

Impact begins when I double what is demanded.

It won't be easy. This battle in our flesh does not need reinforcing from a self-centered culture. Its desire has always been self at the expense of others. This is natural in our everyday life, let alone our church experience on the weekend.

When we come to church services, we still want the songs to be the ones we like. We love it when our preferred preacher is the one bringing the message that day. We love it even more when they speak on our favorite topic. We would love to have curbside valets waiting under a covered driveway with a personal steward inside the lobby waiting with our favorite coffee in his hand.

I know all these things so well because I know *me*. Every single day my flesh keeps coming back to life and trying to make all of life about only me. Maybe that's why Jesus said we have to take up our cross *daily*. (Luke 9:23) It is simply not natural to be selfless. Our desires are already so strong, and our culture reinforces them so much. We must remind ourselves to fight against this. We cannot allow ourselves to entertain the questions, "Do I really have to die to myself? Can't I have it my way?"

If we are not careful, we will give ourselves a pass here and there. We will begin the downward slide into excusing behaviors Jesus would never tolerate. Here again, David Platt cautions us:

> *And this is where we need to pause. Because we are starting to redefine Christianity. We are giving in to the dangerous temptation to take the Jesus of the Bible and twist him into a version of Jesus we are more comfortable with. A nice, middle-class, American Jesus. ... But do you and I realize what we are doing at this point? We are molding Jesus into our image. ... And the danger now is that when we gather in our church buildings to sing and lift up our hands in worship, we may not actually be worshiping the Jesus of the Bible. Instead we may be worshiping ourselves.[9]*

Let's not worship ourselves. Let's worship Jesus. Let's be fully obedient followers. Let's really be disciples. Let's kill the "me monster" that lurks in our hearts.

Jesus told his disciples to give your enemy more than he deserves. If a soldier compels you to go with him one mile, go two. To obey this statement, I have to wrestle with Jesus as much as I have to grapple with me. Jesus, don't you care about me? Don't you understand how hard this is? Why would you ask me to do this?

I have to settle in my heart that Jesus *does* love me, and since He does, there must be something to this command to go the second mile. Maybe He knows that something supernatural happens when I go twice as far as I am required. Perhaps impact begins when I double what was demanded. Maybe *my* healing is found on the second mile. Whatever His reason, I have to believe this: the plan of God is bigger than just my life.

IT'S NOT ABOUT ME.

3

EVERY BELIEVER
A MINISTER

And he gave the apostles, the prophets, the evangelists,
the shepherds and teachers, to equip the saints
for the work of ministry
- Apostle Paul (Ephesians 4:11-12 ESV)

As a pastor and a father of four kids, I've often needed additional income in order to make ends meet. I have had many different jobs–concrete worker, carpenter, civil engineer's apprentice, call center employee, school bus driver, insurance salesman, and emergency medical technician. I do not know what I want to be when I grow up.

Of all those things, one of my favorites was an emergency medical technician. Just like ministry, it is a form of helping people. I loved it. Being on the front lines when someone was sick or injured and making a difference was very fulfilling.

One of the things we were able to do as an ambulance crew was make extra money working local football games. It was easy cash, free football, and free concessions usually given to us by the home team (something my inner fat kid was always thrilled about). Getting paid to watch football and eat food is pretty much the dream job of 85 percent of American men. I was living the dream. Except one day.

On one particular day, I was at home minding my own business and blissfully doing projects around the house when my cell phone rang. It was one of the ambulance service supervisors. He was calling to remind me that I had signed up to work a game and had failed to show up for it. My blissful attitude evaporated. I was completely shocked that I had been so irresponsible.

In order to fill the ambulance service obligation, they had to close one of our stations and send another crewmember to cover my spot until I arrived. I got ready as quickly as possible, threw on my uniform, and drove as fast as I could to get to my assigned spot. I was able to relieve the crew that was there to cover my mistake. Thankfully no emergencies went without service during my absence from duty. Their unit went back in service, and I stayed to work the remainder of the game.

The next day at work I was called into the boss's office. He slid a piece of paper across the desk containing an incident write-up. It cited me for failing to show at my assigned time, further detailing that because I had failed to arrive as scheduled one of our units was taken out of service. Emergency service coverage was diminished as resources had to be reallocated in order for my spot to be covered. I was asked to sign this write-up to document my dereliction of duty. It would be placed in my personnel file and serve as a written history regarding my failure to fulfill my duties.

**Many Christians have not forgotten their duty;
they have never been informed at all.**

Not much came of it because as it stands I am typically very reliable and responsible. I was embarrassed, upset with myself, and quickly willing to sign the paper that documented my failure. I had already beat myself up for being so negligent in failing to show when I was assigned. It weighed heavily on me because I knew someone else had to pick up my slack. Not only that, I placed people at risk in our city for a few minutes because one of our units was pulled from its district. I had disrupted and endangered others because I had forgotten that I was assigned to a duty.

Forgotten Duty

When I failed to show for my shift, it was not because I chose to violate my commitment; I simply forgot about it. The same is true for the church. We have forgotten our duties, responsibilities, tasks, and assignments. To make matters worse, many Christians have not forgotten their duty; they have never been informed at all. They are simply unaware they have been given responsibilities in the Kingdom.

To use a military analogy, every soldier has an assigned duty. For him to fail to perform that duty or desert his brothers is a serious offense. If he simply oversleeps a scheduled shift, he can be disciplined, brought up on charges, or in the worst-case scenario, executed!

Imagine, however, if this soldier or his unit didn't know their duty. What if they were never trained or told? What if there was a battle to which they were supposed to be assigned, but the orders were never received?

Certainly there would be an investigation. They might have to show up to present their case in court, but they certainly could not be held responsible for orders they never received. They would not be considered dishonorable, lazy, or fearful. The responsibility would lie in the failure of the communication system, not the soldiers themselves.

This is the case with much of the church. A communication failure has happened. As a result, we are in a state of affairs as I have described. Many Christians have either forgotten their assignment or have never even been informed of our duty as believers.

In most cases, our churches are filled with people who have never been taught what the Bible actually says regarding their role in the army of God. Most of this can be traced back to the state church being established in Rome. Until that time, the early church understood their responsibilities as believers. They were soldiers in God's army, assigned the task of advancing the kingdom of God against the gates of Hell. Jesus called the church the *ekklésia*–agents of change that would destroy Hell's government. Jesus knew Hell would stand no chance against people who understand that they are soldiers in the army of God when they are trained and willing to perform their duties.

The establishment of the state church changed all this. Ministry was taken from the believer. The Bible was entrusted only to professionals. Laity was replaced with clergy. Only those with special education were considered ministers. Passion became passivity. The movement of the *ekklésia* was brought quickly to a halt.

We can hardly fault the early church for not seeing this coming. Imagine if you and your family lived daily in the threat of prison, torture, or execution in response to your claims that Jesus Christ was Lord. To make this claim meant being marked as a potential target for persecution, prison, or even execution.

They had certainly prayed day after day and year after year for God to remove this threat from their lives. They lived in fear of the worst. Willing to die, lose their families, or suffer whatever it took, they asked God to move in the hearts of those in power for these threats to be removed.

Suddenly the threat was gone. Constantine was converted. Protection was provided and assured under his rule. Revival seemed to sweep the land as Christianity was declared the official religion of the Empire. They were grateful, elated, relieved, and excited to be a part of a nationwide movement. It seemed the kingdoms of this world had become the kingdoms of our God.

It would have been very difficult not to believe that God was behind every aspect of this revolution—that after this period of brutal persecution God had intervened. Significant consequences to the mission of the church would be seen, however, as it became organized and institutionalized. As Daniel Guder and Lois Barrett write,

The emerging priestly order removed church leadership from ordinary existence, as priestly leaders were expected to practice a specialized order of life different from everyone else. Amid this transposition in leadership, then, rank and role increasingly displaced the New Testament experience of gift and charisma.

*The church moved the church into a more settled, established and organized form. ... Many viewed the state's embrace of the church as the hand of God working in church and empire to bring God's reign to earth. ... From a **community** of God's people, the church became a "**place** where" one received grace through a state-sanctioned priesthood[10]*

Church leadership changed. Professionals assumed control of the church. People were no longer taught that the ministry belonged in their hands. Christians under the Roman Empire simply stopped believing the Great Commission was their mission. The soldiers retired from service. Future generations would not even know their duty at all. This strategic move on the part of Hell caused believers to stop their advancement against it. Through a decision that must have seemed like an answer to prayer, believers who had been persecuted, tortured, and killed for their faith now had relief, rest, and apathy.

This state of the church exists still today. Much of the church in America remains sidelined and inactive. While many have forgotten their role, still others have never never been informed that the work of advancing God's kingdom is their primary objective and responsibility.

Leave It To The Pro's

The typical view of the professional clergy is the embodiment of all spiritual gifts into one person. He is our "minister." The pastor or bishop is elevated to a special platform in the body of believers as the one with all the responsibility and knowledge. All others are "ordinary" members of the laity whose jobs involve non-spiritual "secular" work in their professions. They come to church to hear the pastor give them their spiritual food, drop some money into the collection plate, and return to their normal lives. They are completely disconnected from their calling. As a result, what should be accomplished by every ordinary, non-professional person is expected to be accomplished by one full-time professional, the Pastor.

In God's original plan, every single believer is a minister.

Shortly after becoming a campus pastor at CT Church, I had a conversation with a person that illustrates just how strong this idea still holds in church today. We were moving toward a decentralized structure with an emphasis on small groups throughout the week. A man who did not particularly like the direction we were moving came to my office to explain that he and his wife would be leaving the campus. He was very gracious in his speech but was firm in his position against a decentralized ministry.

He explained that what he longed for was a church that had

more gatherings in which the pastor manifested all the gifts of the spirit and "called people out" of the crowd with words of knowledge, words of wisdom, and prophecy. He had previously sat under a pastor where this happened frequently. Under the power of the Spirit, this pastor would call out certain diseases at work in people and then pray for them to be healed.

As I sat listening to him, I realized that his concept of the church was one where the professional pastor contained and manifested every spiritual gift. I began to walk him through my philosophy and beliefs that the entire body working together accomplishes all that God has for them. I encouraged him to pursue allowing God to use him in the same manner his previous pastor had been used. His response perfectly punctuated his view of the divide between clergy and laity. He informed me that this pastor had "dedicated himself full time" to "prayer and fasting." In his opinion, this was how they were able to work in the gifts of the Spirit so powerfully. When I told him that God could use him like this, he rebutted me, saying he had a "regular job" and didn't "have time" to spend with God to that level.

I should not have been stunned, but I was. Sitting in front of me was a Bible-believing Christian who believed he had no role in the body other than to come and hear from the professional and give offerings to the church to enable to pastor reach more people.

It is easy to see why anyone who views the church in this manner would assume a passive role as an attender. They will gather, but never go. Since the pastor is paid to be the specialist in church operations and management, they will sit back and consume rather than contribute. Instead of contributing their part to edify the church, they go to church as passive receivers to be edified. When they could exercise their God-given gifts for the good of the body, they sit back and let the pastor run the show.

This mind-set is pervasive in much of the church today. It is inherited because that's the mind-set of the church from which we came. Our churches today still have the imprints left from Constantine's church. Although we have had substantial reforms, we've inherited much of our methods of leading and governing the church from those ideas.

In the body of Christ many people are not in alignment with God's structure.

Structures That Won't Scale

This mind-set cripples the *ekklésia*! There is simply no way that a single person can grow the church to any substantial size or reach many more than 100 people if all the responsibility of ministry rests squarely on his shoulders. By establishing one gift in the body as the preeminent professional, we have stripped the *ekklésia* of the majority of its workforce. Even if we believe the pastor's role is as a leader, without every other member understanding his rank and role, the Army of God is left with officers only. No army so structured can attack the gates of Hell and move them backward.

Yet in God's original plan, every single believer is a minister, a key part of the *ekklésia*. The pastors aren't responsible for the work but for equipping the believers to do it. In Ephesians 4, Paul clearly outlines this for us:

> *So Christ himself gave the apostles, the prophets, the evangelists, the pastors and teachers, to equip his people for works of service, so that the body of Christ may be built up until we all reach unity in the faith and in the knowledge of the Son of God and become mature, attaining to the whole measure of the fullness of Christ. Then we will no longer be infants, tossed back and forth by the waves, and blown here and there by every wind of teaching and by the cunning and craftiness of people in their deceitful scheming. Instead, speaking the truth in love, we will grow to become in every respect the mature body of him who is the head, that is, Christ. From him the whole body, joined and held together by every supporting ligament, grows and builds itself up in love, as each part does its work. (Ephesians 4:11-15 NIV)*

The word "equip" is the Greek word *katartismos*, which means to fit together or to place in its proper spot. This word has to do with authority and alignment. Soldiers in the military understand alignment under authority. It is because of the authority structure and the command structure that the military is able to mobilize and fulfill mission objectives. In the body of Christ, many people are not in alignment with God's structure. They have never been assigned their proper place.

**Many churches have paid staff doing ministries
that actually belong to the church members.**

Paul says here that the five gifts we often call the "ministers" are given to the church, not to do the ministry but to help everyone find his proper fit, place, and calling in order to do the ministry God has assigned. The five gifts are the *trainers*, not the *doers*.

My dad took me to watch planes when I was young, and since then I have always been fascinated with flying. I hope to be able to fly my own plane someday. Until then, the Federal Aviation Administration says that I can fly a plane provided I bring along a certified flight instructor. The goal of having the instructor with me is for him to train me how to fly the plane without him. Ultimately my goal is to get rid of him and fly by myself. If he flies the plane himself, he is taking advantage of me, milking me for money. If he never teaches me or allows me to take the controls, I would never reach my goal. I would be fairly upset about this.

Yet this is how most Christians operate on a weekly basis. We are perfectly fine having our pastor do all the work. We have been trained to think of him as a pilot when God designed him as a flight instructor. Week after week, we are content to allow him to take us all around the Bible, God, and ministry and bring us back to the same starting spot. We never expect him to train and release us to do it ourselves. We think it is his job to fly the plane, so we never make an attempt to take the controls.

Their job isn't to *do* it. It's to *train* it! Yes, they will also do ministry alongside us because we are *all* ministers. We need, however, to understand that their primary role is to show us how to do it and release us to do it. They are equippers, not doers. If my instructor did all the flying, I would find another one. Likewise, if our church leaders are not challenging and equipping us to do the ministry, we should find another Apostle, Prophet, Evangelist, Pastor, or Teacher who expects us to become all that God intends for us to be.

Some Christians grow old but never grow up in their faith.
They believe they are mature in Christ
but are simply aged infants.

Many pastors face fierce resistance when they begin to challenge their people to do more ministry. They have congregants who think, "That's what we pay you for." They try to train and equip, but the concept is foreign to many in the church. All they have ever known is the "preacher" being their "minister." As a result, much of the church's money is spent on paid staff to do ministry rather than funding ministries led by the congregation. Many churches have paid staff doing ministries that actually belong to the church members. Churches under this paradigm have very limited growth. Funds are used for salaries instead of schools to train people to do ministry.

If we are ever able to restore the expectation for the fivefold gifts to become trainers of ministers, Paul begins to describe what will happen in the church. He says:

1. The body of Christ will be built up.
2. We will reach unity in the faith and knowledge of Jesus.
3. We will attain the fullness of Christ.
4. We won't be infants tossed around by bad doctrine.
5. We will be the mature body of Christ.
6. The body will build itself up in love **as each member does its part.**

This is a description of very few churches because few people are doing their part in ministry. Instead they are content to assemble each week thinking the pastor's role is to dispense the knowledge they need to grow in maturity, overcome the world, and walk in God's blessing. Without assuming the role of ministry, we will never see the six things Paul describes. As a result, some Christians grow old but never grow up in their faith. They believe they are mature in Christ but are simply aged infants.

It's time to remember we have a duty, an assignment, a place in the body of Christ to be a part of the *ekklésia*. Only then will the gates of Hell shake against the power of an advancing army of God. Peter says it this way:

Kings and Priests

*But you are a chosen generation, a **royal priesthood**, a holy nation, His own special **people**, that you may proclaim the praises of Him who called you out of darkness* *into His marvelous light. (1 Peter 2:9 NKJV)*

This verse is so powerful, and Peter states it so clearly. We have all been chosen. We have all been invited to become the *ekklésia*. Peter makes this bold assertion to his audience: We are ***all*** kings. We are ***all*** priests. Every single believer is a minister. *You* are a minister. Let that sink in!

**"Thy Kingdom come" was not
simply their prayer; it was their purpose.**

In the Old Testament, only one select group of people was able to perform the functions of the priesthood. Yet in the New Testament believers understood that their function and role had dramatically shifted. As believers they had been promoted to a place of kingship in the body of Christ. As part of the *ekklésia*, we have the rights, privileges, and expectations to be part of the ruling body in the kingdom. "Thy Kingdom come" was not simply their prayer; it was their purpose.

This fact alone was incredible, but Peter continues. He informs them they have also been made priests! Imagine how this must have astounded the Jewish believers. They knew clearly from the pattern of the Old Testament that priests had special access to God. Priests had the ability and the assignment to be close to Him, performing works of ministry. Priests were able to be near to Him, speak to Him, and speak *for* Him.

Having lost this clear understanding today, we suffer the

Constantinian paralysis. Even as we read this verse over and over, we miss the implications. Constantine's order re-established the professional, limited priesthood. The non-professional believer was excluded from his role as priest and given a procedure to come close to God. Once again he was required to come through a person who had special access—the priest or "Father."

This idea is still prevalent in the church today. People in churches everywhere somehow have the idea that their pastor has a special phone sitting on his desk that is a hotline to God. They believe this phone exists only for the pastor and somehow they need to go through the pastor in order to speak with God.

It is as though they imagine when the pastor picks up this special phone God is always waiting on the other end. So when someone is sick in the hospital, they call their priest or their pastor. They forget they, too, are priests and as such also have special access to God. If they talk to Him, He hears them. He answers them.

I'm always astounded by believers that feel I have a special access to God they do not possess. It is such a limiting idea. God hears them, too! In fact, God uses some of the people in my church more in the gift of healing than He uses me! Why wouldn't you want that person to pray for you instead of me?

The only reason we perpetuate this process is ignorance. People simply do not understand that they, too, are kings and priests; that they have access to God; and that they are the ministers.

Peter continues this verse by saying that we are "God's own special people." This word he uses for people is the Greek word *laós*. This is the very word from which we derive the English word "laity."

Guess who are the special "people." Guess who are the priests. Not only the clergy but also the laity.

Reporting for Duty

At some point we have to come to understand and believe this. We have to realize that we are all ministers. We need to show up at our assigned posts and perform our duty. The army has been stripped of its soldiers far too long. It's time for the *ekklésia* to move forward again.

**It's time to realize we are royals
and stop behaving as peasants.**

This is the very thing Satan fears. If we ever report back to our posts and resume our duties, we will be unstoppable. I believe Satan fears this more than anything and is doing everything he can to prevent it. He wants to keep the laity from realizing that Ephesians 4 and 1 Peter 2:9 contain the solution to a triumphant church. He knows that this idea, if fully embraced, would unleash an army of warriors on the world that has been silenced since Constantine! Satan cannot afford for you and me to understand who we really are.

I'm reminded of a scene in the kids movie, *A Bug's Life*. The ants are terrorized by grasshoppers who demand that the ants continue to harvest food and give it to the grasshoppers. At one point, the grasshoppers face a setback as the ants begin to raise a rebellion against their reign of terror. The leader of the grasshoppers (Hopper) is challenged by one of his subordinates who thinks they should excuse this one act of defiance. He asks Hopper just to let it go. After all, they are tired, and this is only one little revolt by the ants. His theory is they will get enough food from them next time.

Hopper lets the rest of the group in on a big secret. Their greatest weapon against the ants is fear. They have to continue to make them afraid because the ants outnumber them 100 to 1. Hopper informs the grasshoppers that if the ants ever figure out they outnumber the grasshoppers, their reign of terror and free food provided by the ants are over. Hopper says, "If they ever figure that out, there goes our way of life." Inspired, the grasshoppers go back to instill a new level of fear in the ants.

This is a great depiction of the church. For too long we have allowed only the professionals to be the priests. We have missed our ministry. We gather, but never go. As a result, Satan remains in power, terrorizing and destroying the people we love. We can easily defeat him, but only if we remember that we are the *ekklésia*, that we are the ministers of Ephesians 4, and that we are Kings-Priests of 1 Peter 2. Jesus said "upon this rock" he would build a church that Hell wouldn't stand a chance against.

It's time to realize we are royals and stop behaving as peasants. It is time to stop cowering and live as conquerors. We are more than able to do the work for which Jesus called us.

We continue to behave just as the children of Israel. They sent spies to confirm what God had already said was true about the land into which he was sending them. Upon seeing the people who lived there, they cowered in fear. They compared their size to the giants rather than compare the giants to their God. They said:

We seemed like grasshoppers in our own eyes, and we looked the same to them.
(Numbers 13:33 NIV)

Not only did they suppose they were small, they even gave voice to what they supposed the enemy might have thought about them as well. They were defeated before they ever returned to give their report to the leaders of Israel. While it is easy to pass judgement on them from this point, we often exhibit the same beliefs and behaviors today. It is time to fight this "small me" mentality that has been in God's people since the wilderness. We are more than able. He is with us.

Our family had a Black Labrador Retriever named Camo for several years. He was massive. He looked more like a small bear than a dog. Our daughter Alexan has a very small dog Shammy that is loud, feisty, and defensive. Although Camo could have swallowed this dog without chewing, he would shrink into a corner when Shammy barked at him. It was hilarious to watch the interactions. The small dog was picking a fight it could not win, and the big dog was cowering from a fight he could not lose. He was 10 times her size, but He didn't know it or believe it.

If we ever become serious about being the *ekklésia*, and if we ever decide to fulfill the role Jesus intended for us, we will revolutionize the world for God.

Even now Satan is working to keep you and me convinced that we are incapable of fulfilling the great commission. He is keeping an illusion in front of us so we will remain silent and still. "Keep quiet; stay seated," he encourages. "Besides, ministry isn't your job anyway. This guy is just trying to get you to work for the church for free." Another voice is calling you though. Deep down inside you *know* what you are called to do.

You are the *ekklésia*. You are a King. You are a Priest.

YOU ARE A MINISTER OF THE GOSPEL OF JESUS CHRIST.

4

IT'S UP TO ME

Action springs not from thought,
but from a readiness for responsibility.
- Dietrich Bonhoeffer

From the time I sincerely gave my life to Jesus at age 14, I began to have a desperate desire to be in "full-time" ministry. While many people run from their calling, I cried many tears at the altar asking Jesus to give me one. I wanted an opportunity to give my life to work in church. I did everything I could to make that dream a reality. I served as a volunteer at our church as if I were paid staff. My youth pastor, Thomas Hale, used me for everything from taking out the trash to working on Excel spreadsheets to collecting money for our ski trip. I had no idea what ministry looked like. I didn't know what was required. I just kept showing up.

My faithfulness and commitment opened the door for me for my dream. I was invited to come on staff at another church as a paid intern. I did not land the position because of my knowledge or qualifications but because of my diligence and work ethic. This church brought me on the team with the intention to train me up to become the youth pastor as they transitioned their existing youth pastor, Preston Smith, to another role. I was thrilled beyond belief. This was my dream! Until I had my first nightmare situation.

Our young adults ministry, which I was jointly overseeing with our youth pastor, met in small groups throughout the city each week. In one of the very first meetings I attended, the leader, who was twice my age, became very frustrated that many of the group failed to show up that night. He expressed his frustration regarding those absent members of the group with those of us who were in attendance that night. Name by name he called out people who were not in attendance, citing their absence as evidence that they were uncommitted to Jesus and the church. Verily I say unto thee, I was uncomfortable.

Even though I was brand new to church staff and ministry, I instinctively knew that this well-meaning fellow was sowing seeds of discord and division within our church. I knew someone should say something. Someone should do something.

Like any fine upstanding minister, I did the responsible thing. I passed the buck to our youth pastor. In no uncertain terms, I vented my frustration to him. I questioned how we could allow such a person on our team. I detailed the offense this leader had committed. I made sure my youth pastor knew what I thought. I told him exactly what I thought he should do: he should call the guy in and do something about this egregious offense. "This is not right," I fumed, "something has to be done." I felt I was justified in my righteous anger.

My expectation was twofold: First, that the youth pastor

would agree with me. Second, that he should call this not-so-gentle gentleman in and confront him concerning his behavior, giving him a taste of his own medicine. He met 50 percent of my expectations.

First, he agreed with me. This man was in the wrong, and it needed to be addressed. As to the second expectation, however, he said something utterly horrifying, "You need to take him to lunch and confront it."

I don't know exactly what I said, but I felt like saying, "I'm sorry. I resign." I had no experience in dealing with situations like this. To fully understand the terror I felt in this moment, I need tell you a little something about myself.

I am a white person. Stark White. I am only ever two colors. Lobster Red from sunburn or Ghost White. I don't even try to tan. It's not worth it. I will burn, endure misery, itch, shed my dead skin, and be right back where I started. So when you see me, I normally look pale–maybe even frightened. Yet when my leader told me I had to be the one to confront the sin, I believe I turned so white that any-one who saw me would have mistaken me for the angel of the Lord.

I thought I had brought *him* a problem to deal with, and he had just turned it right back on me. I had hoped that he would be the one to do the dirty work. I thought he would confront the situation while I sat in the bleachers with soda and popcorn in hand. I hoped he would take responsibility for what needed to be done, but that is not how it happened. I had opened my big mouth about injustice, and here I was being asked to be the one to take care of it. "You want *me* to handle it?" I asked. A nod "yes." Then silence. I had my orders.

So I handled it. I took the guy to lunch. I had no idea what I was doing. I was extremely nervous and thought I would feel better if I just got it out in the open. Because I wanted to get it over with, immediately upon being seated, ordering our drinks, and before even reviewing the menus, I confronted him. I wasted no time building rapport. I applied zero principles from the classic, *How To Win Friends and Influence People*. I simply blurted out, "Hey, the reason I asked you to lunch is to talk about what happened at small group. The way you talked about those members of our group without them being present was wrong."

I did what I was told to do. I fixed it. Literally the end of discussion. My talking points took less than three minutes to complete. With nothing much more to say, we awkwardly ate our lunch and said our goodbyes.

Before I had even made it back to the church office, he had already phoned the youth pastor yelling and screaming, asking if I had been placed over him in authority. He stated very clearly he had no intentions of letting some young kid tell him what to do. A *second* meeting was called. Before we talked, we prayed. That was a really good idea. Perhaps my youth pastor should have told me to lead with that before my previous meeting and we would not have found ourselves in this new awkward one. After prayer we had a time to work through the situation. My youth pastor did a masterful job leading the meeting. The situation was resolved, and we left as ministry partners and friends. I knew he could do it. He should have listened to me the first time.

Truthfully I have never really enjoyed dealing with conflict.

While I have developed skills that are helpful in dealing with difficult situations, it is still not natural to me. Growing up, much of our conflict resolution at home involved a rug and a broom, so to this day I do not enjoy confrontation. I prefer that someone else have the hard conversations. I am so much better at good cop.

This is how it is with everything in life, isn't it? We prefer for someone else to do the dirty work, the heavy lifting–for them to take the brunt of the heat or situation. We would prefer to skirt by on the outside of conflict and get to be the comforter rather than the confronter. We would rather someone else "adult" for us, manage our checkbook, make our career decisions, do our job, or mow the grass. We'd also rather someone else do the ministry.

It does not work that way. We each have a role and responsibility. Just as I had the realization that confronting this youth leader was my responsibility, we all need to adopt the mind-set, "Ministry is up to me."

No one else is coming to do what God has given *me* to do.

As we discussed in the previous chapter, Peter says the distinctions of the Levitical priesthood have been set aside. Now we are *all* kings and priests. We are all in "full-time" ministry. I have been sent to Earth, in this season and in this country, for a specific purpose that is unique to me. God needs me to do the ministry He called *me* to do. He needs you to do the ministry He called *you* to do.

The new belief about ministry must be this: It's up to me. What God is asking of the believers in this world is up to me. No one else is coming to do what God has given *me* to do. If you and I do not do the work assigned to us by Jesus, no one else will.

When I spoke with my youth pastor, Preston, I really did think it was his job to confront that guy. I felt that since he was the pastor–the boss–he should be the one to make the corrections, but he saw it differently. Since I was the one to witness the offense, it was my duty to deal with it, not his. It was only his duty to get involved if I could not win my brother back on my own.

Most of us have never realized that our pastor is not our "minister." We call him to do all the ministry. We believe that's what we pay him for. Yet that's not true according to the Bible. Scripture reveals that their purpose is to give you the tools necessary for you to be ministers of the grace of Jesus. Remember Ephesians 4 states that Christ gave the five gifts of apostle, prophet, evangelist, pastor, and teacher to the church, not to *do* the ministry but to *equip* the ministers. In other words, your leaders in your church should be training you, equipping you, and expecting you to do the ministry. It's not up to them. It's up to you.

Take a moment to process this idea: The ministry that God has called the church to is **my** responsibility. No one else is coming. No one else is responsible for what God has called me to do. It is up to me.

Good Works

I love quoting Ephesians 2:8-9 when I share the gospel with people. Most people love to point out that they are good persons. They base their salvation on their ability to do and be good. This passage makes it so clear that our salvation is **not a result of our works** but because of the grace of Christ.

> *For it is by grace you have been saved, through faith - and this is not from yourselves, it is the gift of God - not by works, so that no one can boast. (Ephesians 2:8-9 NIV)*

We love to quote this passage, and we should! It gives us such a clear picture of the grace and goodness of God and how salvation is NOT tied to anything we do. It's not of our own efforts. Nothing we can do will get us saved; however, this is not the end of this passage. It continues:

> *For we are God's handiwork, created in Christ Jesus **to do good works**, which God prepared in advance for us to do. (Ephesians 2:10 NIV)*

Did you catch that? Our works do nothing to save us. You and I had nothing to do with our salvation. It is Jesus alone. Now that we are saved, however, there is a new expectation. We were created new in Christ Jesus by Christ Jesus "***to do good works***." We were not saved *by* good works, but we were saved *to* good works.

The scripture further states that God prepared these works in advance for you. Imagine this: Before God even created you, He created work for you to do. Ministry. An assignment. Responsibility. Not for anyone else. Not for your pastor. You.

And guess what. If you don't do those works, it is highly

likely they will not get done. God made you perfect to do these works. He placed gifts in you that are perfect for these works. He put you in this world, in this place, at this time, and in the relationships you have to do these works. These works cannot be done by anyone else. Say this with me: "It's up to me."

We must recognize the situation and shoulder the responsibility. It is not the job of the pastors to do the ministry. It is *our* job to do the ministry. If we don't realize that every believer is a minister, the job will not get done. If we do not answer the call to make disciples, no one else will! No one else is coming to take the responsibility that belongs to us.

The analogy of our last chapter was an army that had forgotten or had never been informed of its duty. If entire armies went Absent Without Official Leave (AWOL), imagine the atrocities committed by aggressors. Imagine the hurt and pain on mass scale because good men did nothing.

God has no Plan B. He didn't create an alternative plan just in case we don't step up to the plate and do what He assigned for us to do.

Until now you may never have considered yourself called to full-time ministry, yet our whole life is ministry. We are strategically formed and placed for the purpose God has for us. Now that we know, now that we have received our orders, it is our duty to act and carry out God's plan for this world. Say this with me: "It's up to me."

To think that God has a purpose for our lives that only we can complete is a bit of a heavy realization. Although God is omnipotent, He has chosen a plan that limits Him to our cooperation with His plan. He has relegated the outcome of this world to the church, His chosen people, the *ekklésia*. This group of people is responsible to pray that His Kingdom come on Earth as it is in Heaven and then make it so with His help.

God has no Plan B. He didn't create an alternative plan just in case we don't step up to the plate and do what He assigned us to do. No one else is coming. There is no other solution. There is no other way. He is waiting for us to fulfill the Great Commission. He is waiting for us to do the ministry.

For years we have seen the business of the church as the responsibility of one man, the pastor. Church was his job, and we had our own. We would show up to church on the weekend to see what he had prepared for us. We would listen politely, give our offerings, and go about "our" business. But whose business is the kingdom? Whose ministry is it? It is our business, our ministry. It's up to me.

With that in mind, let us ponder some questions about what happens at church on the weekend and in the church throughout the week:

- Whose job is it to meet new people on the weekend?
- Whose job is it to disciple people?
- Whose job is it to witness to people?
- Whose job is it to set up for events?
- Whose job is it to make sure people are being called when

they miss church?

- Whose job is it to visit people in the hospital?
- Whose job is it to pray with people?
- Whose job is it to organize events?
- Whose job is it to work the nursery?
- Whose job is it to counsel people?
- Whose job is it to visit the elderly?
- Whose job is it to get new people connected?
- Whose job is it to coordinate volunteers?

Say this with me: "It's up to me."

The Buck Stops Here

In the old west, poker was a popular game in the saloons. Players were often suspected of cheating by "dirty dealing" while handing out cards to the other players. In an effort to minimize the cheating, players traded turns dealing cards to the other players at the table. The marker to keep track of whose turn it was to deal was a knife with a buckhorn for the handle. The marker was called a "buck."

Even with the rotation of dealer responsibility, however, the combination of alcohol, firearms, and suspicion still led to many arguments and shootouts. Many players worried that they would be accused of cheating when they dealt the cards, so they would pass on their turn to deal. Avoiding the responsibility, they would "pass the buck."

This phrase became synonymous with avoiding responsibility and letting someone else deal with difficult situations. Conversely the saying, "The Buck Stops Here" became synonymous with someone taking the responsibility to deal with tough circumstances and refusing to make someone else handle it or blame others. President Harry Truman popularized the phrase with a sign on his desk in the Oval Office that read "The Buck Stops Here." He was saying, "I take full responsibility for it all. It's up to me."

We have too many people in the church who are passing the buck, hoping that someone else will do the hard work.

Imagine how much more powerful the body of Christ in the world would be if all Christians (1) knew their responsibility and (2) accepted it. What if we all said, "The Buck Stops Here"?

We would have Christians who wouldn't have to be begged or badgered into serving in the local church. We would have no shortage of volunteers and leaders of ministries. We would have people starting parachurch ministries in their cities, meeting the needs of people in the community, and leading many to Jesus. Pastors would have to ask people to slow down and take a break as they run toward the call of God on their lives. Instead of feeling as though they are pushing a resistant group of people up a hill, they would feel as though they are chasing them down the hill as they charge the gates of Hell.

We have too many people in the church who are passing the buck, hoping that someone else will do the hard work, have the hard conversation, or do what they are simply just too uncommitted to do. Pastors all over the country are praying right now for someone to say, "The buck stops here," "I'll take responsibility," "Pick me," "I'll do it," or "Just give me a green light and I'll run with the vision." They are looking for a group of people who will say, "I'm not sitting back and waiting for someone else to take care of this. I'll do it. It's up to me!"

Reluctant Neighbors

The unwillingness to assume responsibility is not new. It is recorded throughout the Bible. This reluctance is recorded in the story of the Good Samaritan. In Luke chapter 10, Jesus is confronted with the question "Who is my neighbor?"

On one occasion an expert in the law stood up to test Jesus. "Teacher," he asked, "what must I do to inherit eternal life?" "What is written in the Law?" he replied. "How do you read it?" He answered, "'Love the Lord your God with all your heart and with all your soul and with all your strength and with all your mind'; and, 'Love your neighbor as yourself.'" "You have answered correctly," Jesus replied. "Do this and you will live." But he wanted to justify himself, so he asked Jesus, "And who is my neighbor?" In reply Jesus said: "A man was going down from Jerusalem to Jericho, when he was attacked by robbers. They stripped him of his clothes, beat him and went away, leaving him half dead. A priest happened to be going down the same road, and when he saw the man, he passed by on the other side. So too, a Levite, when he came to the place and saw him, passed by on the other side. But a Samaritan, as he traveled, came where the man was; and when he saw him, he took pity on him. He went to him and bandaged his wounds, pouring on oil and wine. Then he put the man on his own donkey, brought him to an inn and took care of him. The next day he took out two denarii and gave them to the innkeeper. 'Look after him,' he said, 'and when I return, I will reimburse you for any extra expense you may have.' "Which of these three do you think was a neighbor to the man who fell into the hands of robbers?" The expert in the law replied, "The one who had mercy on him." Jesus told him, "Go and do likewise." (Luke 10:25-37 NIV)

The man asked Jesus to tell him who *was* his neighbor. This is a limiting question. What he was really asking was "What is the minimum I can do?" He wanted to know how little he could get by with. To define who was his neighbor also defined who was *not* his neighbor.

Jesus in His wisdom turned the tables on the man. While the man was asking how he could qualify for Heaven, Jesus wanted to confront his heart. The man wanted to know who *was* his neighbor; Jesus wanted him to *be* one.

Jesus revealed the heart of the man and the fact that he was looking for a way *out* of responsibility, not a way *into* it. He wanted to be excused from rather than opt in to responsibility. As you read this chapter and this story in Luke, ask yourself this question, "Would I rather know who is my neighbor or look for a way to be one?"

As a Second Mile Leader, hopefully you are looking for ways to be a neighbor and to step into ministry opportunities. Let's ask some probing questions:

- When church service ends, do you cut out as soon as possible or do you hang around to see what assistance is needed?
- Do you enter and exit right at the beginning and ending of services or do you show up early and stay late, attempting to connect with others?
- Are you personally sharing your faith with people?
- Are you inviting people or hoping someone else does?
- Do you shoulder the burden Christ had for the lost or are you simply saved for the benefits?
- Are you more concerned with your rights or your responsibilities?
- Have you completed the membership processes for your church?
- Have you engaged in serving or are you just sitting?

Our priorities and attitudes are revealed by our actions. As we have seen, every believer is a minister, yet many believers are frequently Missing In Action when it comes to the cause of Jesus Christ and our service in the local church. When it comes to responsibility, many believers duck their heads, look the other way, or simply don't show up, thereby hoping to avoid commitment.

I remember the following proverbial story from middle school. One of my teachers read it aloud one day. I thought how cleverly the words were spun together and how much meaning was conveyed through this short little blurb about dealing with responsibility. It's a short story about four people named Everybody, Somebody, Anybody, and Nobody.

> *There was an important job to be done, and Everybody was sure that Somebody would do it. Anybody could have done it, but Nobody did it. Somebody got angry about that because it was Everybody's job. Everybody thought that Anybody could do it, but Nobody realized that Everybody wouldn't do it. It ended up that Everybody blamed Somebody when Nobody did what Anybody could have done.*

Isn't this a sad truth regarding the church, and isn't it time that it's no longer true? Say this with me: "It's up to me."

Let's stop waiting. Let's remember we are enlisted men and women in the army of God. Hell has billions captive, and we are the only ones who can do something about it.

If we refuse our duty to act, it is desertion. In the "real-world" military, desertion is met with court martial and a punishment of prison or even death. In Ezekiel God also has some very strong language regarding following through on our assignments:

"When I say to a wicked person, 'You will surely die,' and you do not warn them or speak out to dissuade them from their evil ways in order to save their life, that wicked person will die for their sin, and I will hold you accountable for their blood." (Ezekiel 3:18 NIV)

I will hold you accountable for their blood!

When we stand before God, we will have to give an account for what we did and what we did not do! Let's do what He called us to do! Let's remember we are authorized and empowered to fight the enemy on behalf of those dying in their sins. If we refuse to engage, their blood is on our hands.

Send Me

As we bring this chapter to a close, consider whether or not you have fully engaged as a leader in the body of Christ. Where is your commitment level? What is your life all about? You? Your personal pursuits? Your own Kingdom? Or is it about God and His Kingdom and His purpose in your life?

If it's not aligned properly, let's fix that right now. Pray and ask God to change your mind and heart so you can begin to step into the purpose and plan He has for you. Let's echo the words of Isaiah when he heard the call of God for someone who would go for Him.

It was in the year King Uzziah died that I saw the Lord. He was sitting on a lofty throne, and the train of his robe filled the Temple. Attending him were mighty seraphim, each having six wings. With two wings they covered their faces, with two they covered their feet, and with two they flew. They were calling out to each other, "Holy, holy, holy is the LORD of Heaven's Armies! The whole earth is filled with his glory!" Their voices shook the Temple to its foundations, and the entire building was filled with smoke. Then I said, "It's all over! I am doomed, for I am a sinful man. I have filthy lips, and I live among a people with filthy lips. Yet I have seen the King, the LORD of Heaven's Armies." Then one of the seraphim flew to me with a burning coal he had taken from the altar with a pair of tongs. He touched my lips with it and said, "See, this coal has touched your lips. Now your guilt is removed, and your sins are forgiven." Then I heard the Lord asking, "Whom should I send as a messenger to this people? Who will go for us?" **I said, "Here I am. Send me."** *(Isaiah 6:1-8 NLT)*

As God was then, He is still searching for people who will answer His call. He is looking for someone to hear His call, share His heartbeat, and say, "Here I Am. Send Me." Are you one who will say that? Are you ready for God to say "Go"? Can you pre-decide right now that you will say to God, "Whatever you ask, my answer in advance is yes"?

Are you ready to do anything regardless of what it is? Are you willing to serve in any way? From cleaning toilets to administration, teaching, preaching, witnessing, hosting, calling, leading, or praying, are you willing to say, "I'll do it, God! Send me!"?

No one else can do what God has assigned you to do. You were created in Christ Jesus to do good works that God prepared in advance for you to do. Will you do those? Will you decide that you won't watch and wait, hoping that someone else will pick up the task and the responsibility so you don't have to? Say this with me:

IT'S UP TO ME.

5

MULTIPLY MINISTRY

Are you jealous for my sake? I wish that all the LORD's
people were prophets and that the LORD would put his
Spirit upon them all!
- Moses (Numbers 11:29 NLT)

I think I have had career attention deficit hyperactivity dis-
order (ADHD) most of my life. I have been a Jack-of-all-trades,
working in many different types of jobs. I suppose it kept me from
boredom, but the main objective was to find a way to pay the bills.
When you choose working on staff at a church as your career, you
typically will need a second job to help put food on the table. I have
had many adventures along the way. During one of those attempts
to make a living, I began working for a company that specialized in
life insurance and helping people prepare for retirement.

Being in a profession that helped people buy and sell stocks,
from time to time people would come to the office excited about the
next big thing. A friend of a friend of a friend had told them about a
new company whose stock was going to skyrocket in price. They ad-
vised them to hurry so they could get in on the ground floor. If they

invested all their money, they would be rich in just a year or two. They would ask us to help them invest their money in this company. What happened next was usually conversation to attempt to get them back to reality and away from this type of investment strategy.

Significant risk and reward potential exist with investing like that. On the one hand, if the company were to be wildly successful, you could indeed become very wealthy. You would laugh all the way to the bank, depositing your millions as you made fun of all the people who refused to believe in your plan. On the other hand, if the company were to flounder or even fail, you would become very broke. With your investment gone, you might be the illustration of choice in a seminar on wise investment strategies.

We did not invest directly in single stocks for people at our company; instead, we used a tool called mutual funds to help people build their retirement assets. This tool allows you to make investments in a single account while the account manager chooses many different stocks in which to invest the money. Even though you might make small investments, they would be diversified, spread out over many underlying stocks. If one company were to underperform or fail, all would not be lost. With your money allocated in different investments, your risk is lowered.

This strategy is a solution to the old proverbial illustration about not "putting all your eggs in one basket." If everything you have is in that one particular basket and you drop it, all is lost. If, however, you have multiple people helping you carry the eggs in different baskets and one is lost, you still have other baskets with eggs remaining in them. Risk is lowered; all is not lost.

Diversify Ministry

For many years, the church has put all its eggs in the ministry basket called the pastor. He was the professional minister in which all the gifts were concentrated. He was expected to be the preacher, teacher, and evangelist; he was expected to be the greeter at the door; he was the person with mercy, exhortation, and the gift of prophecy; he was the church's Jack-of-all-trades.

This expectation on the pastor is not only stressful but also unbiblical. Allowing or expecting one person to fulfill all the ministry of the church slows the work and plan of God. Our cities remain unreached as members take passive roles, expecting their pastor to do all and be all.

There is something spiritually dangerous about this idea. Just like putting all our eggs in one basket, ministry built around a single individual means the work of the church rises and falls on this one person. Add a dynamic leader to the church and it flourishes; remove that leader from the church and it struggles to survive. Having all the gifts concentrated in one individual exposes the church to high risk. If the main leader dies, fails, or moves, the church suffers needlessly.

How many times have we seen entire ministries come crashing down because they were built around a single individual? Remove the pastor from the picture; take away his leadership, his style, his communication, and his charisma and the entire ministry crumbles. For churches to become all God intends, we need a strategy to diversify leadership into other people and set up lines of succession should something happen the the point leader.

The United States government even mitigates its leadership risk by having a designated survivor moved to a secure location during the State of the Union speech. When all branches of government are in one room, a plan is in place to sustain the government in the event of a worst-case-scenario terrorist attack. This designated survivor would be tasked with rebuilding the government and sustaining our democracy if the unthinkable ever happened.

Maximize Impact

For too long the church has believed God's plan is to have a single individual responsible for the ministry of the church. When the work of God is concentrated around a single individual, it is minimized. Our churches remain small, and our cities remain unreached. We have minimal impact. This certainly does not represent the *ekklésia*. This is not God's plan for the church. By allowing this model to be perpetuated, professional ministers are expected to carry a load they were never meant to carry. The ministry of the church grinds to a halt.

In Acts chapter 6 the early church is growing rapidly. Many people are being saved and beginning to follow Jesus. As the church continues to grow, problems begin to emerge. The growth of the church actually becomes a threat to the growth of the church. In order to continue to grow, leadership changes need to be made. Watch what happens:

> *In those days when the number of disciples was increasing, the Hellenistic Jews among them complained*

*against the Hebraic Jews because their widows were being overlooked in the daily distribution of food. So the Twelve gathered all the disciples together and said, "It would not be right for us to neglect the ministry of the word of God in order to wait on tables. Brothers and sisters, choose seven men from among you who are known to be full of the Spirit and wisdom. We will turn this responsibility over to them and will give our attention to prayer and the ministry of the word." This proposal pleased the whole group. They chose Stephen, a man full of faith and of the Holy Spirit; also Philip, Procorus, Nicanor, Timon, Parmenas, and Nicolas from Antioch, a convert to Judaism. They presented these men to the apostles, who prayed and laid their hands on them. **So the word of God spread. The number of disciples in Jerusalem increased rapidly,** and a large number of priests became obedient to the faith. (Acts 6:1-7 NIV)*

Problems were happening because the church was growing. As our churches grow, things become more complicated. An increase in people means an increase in problems. Pastors become distracted from their vision to reach people by the people they have reached. Once fire starters, they become firefighters. The needs in the church begin to multiply. Pastors are pulled in hundreds of directions. Growth can no longer be sustained.

When pastors leave the ministry God has assigned to them in order to do the ministry God has assigned to others, the church can no longer grow.

This was the problem in the early church. The apostles were being asked to deal with disputes, settle issues, and solve problems. The apostles assessed the problem and noted it was a real situation that required a solution. Something must be done. But what? And by whom?

Notice the wisdom God gave them to deal with this problem: "It would not be right for us to neglect the ministry of the word of God in order to wait on tables. Brothers and sisters, choose seven men from among you who are known to be full of the Spirit and wisdom. We will turn this responsibility over to them and will give our attention to prayer and the ministry of the word." (Acts 6:3-4)

The apostles realized that if they stopped doing what they were called to do to solve problems, the church would no longer grow. They also knew that if someone did not solve problems, the church would not grow. They realized something must be done, but they made two observations: First they realized the need should be addressed. Second they realized this was not a need *they* should address.

Here is where most churches get stuck. They expect the staff or the pastor to meet the needs and solve the problems of the congregation. Pastors do their best to help their people, but growth becomes stifled and churches stay small.

The apostles never said the job was *beneath* them. They stated it was not *right* for them. Real leaders would never claim to be above serving the church in any way. They are willing to do whatever and whenever in order to help the church. But just because they *can* does not mean they *should*. When pastors leave the ministry God has assigned to them in order to do the ministry God has assigned to others, the church can no longer grow.

The early church had a need in its body. They enabled those with the right gifting to do the right job. Are you doing the right job? Have you found your fit and function? The church begins to flourish when each person finds what God has uniquely designed him to do. This is part of becoming a Second Mile Leader.

Part Of The Whole

God never intended to concentrate all the gifts into a single individual called "pastor." The New Testament describes the church as a body. Just as a body has many parts with specific functions, each person in the church has a unique part to play. Every person has a need he can meet. Each has something to share with others. Whatever is your part to play in the body, you should discover it and then do it!

Just as a body, though one, has many parts, but all its many parts form one body, so it is with Christ. For we were all baptized by one Spirit so as to form one body— whether Jews or Gentiles, slave or free—and we were all given the one Spirit to drink. Even so the body is not made up of one part but of many. Now if the foot should

say, "Because I am not a hand, I do not belong to the body," it would not for that reason stop being part of the body. And if the ear should say, "Because I am not an eye, I do not belong to the body," it would not for that reason stop being part of the body. If the whole body were an eye, where would the sense of hearing be? If the whole body were an ear, where would the sense of smell be? But in fact God has placed the parts in the body, every one of them, just as he wanted them to be. If they were all one part, where would the body be? As it is, there are many parts, but one body.
(1 Corinthians 12:12-20 NIV)

The body is not one part, but many! If our foot decided it didn't like being a foot and detached itself from our body, what would happen? It would die! Feet are gross! But detached and dead feet are even grosser! Without feet our bodies are disabled, unable to move freely as God intended. We need our feet.

You were never intended to *compete* with the person beside you but to *complete* the person beside you.

The body of Christ needs every body part, too! For it to be all God intended, every person needs to discover his design and fulfill his destiny. Many people never perform the ministry God gave them simply because they have never discovered what it is. When people discover how God uniquely designed them, they need to be able to accept that role as God-given.

Some people discover their design but reject it. They are discontent with the gift God has given them because they see it as less than the gift of someone else. Our society loves to maximize the gifts that get the spotlight and minimize those that happen backstage. As a result many people choose not to offer the gift God has given them because they do not see its value. Paul warns us against this gift envy in verse 19 when he says, *"If they were all one part, where would the body be?"* The truth is there would not be a body at all.

Can you imagine a body that was just one huge eye? It would have great vision but little mobility. It would have perfect ability to see what needs to be done, but it would be without hands and feet to do anything about it.

**Our culture celebrates our individualism,
but God celebrates our togetherness.**

In the last chapter we talked about the works He created you to do. You're perfect for those assignments, but if we spend our time judging our gifting by someone else's calling, we will always feel like a failure. The old allegory says, "Everyone is a genius, but if you judge a fish by its ability to climb a tree, it will live its whole life believing that it is stupid." People are deceived into believing they have little to offer simply because they do not possess the same giftings as the person next to them. This uniqueness is by design. You were never intended to compete with the person beside you but to complete the person beside you.

For God to complete His work through the church, every part of the body needs to function to its fullest. Our culture celebrates our individualism, but God celebrates our *togetherness*. We are not simply individuals; instead, we are individual members who belong to one another. Ephesians 4:16 (NIV) says, *"From him the whole body, joined and held together by every supporting ligament, grows and builds itself up in love, **as each part does its work**."* Why do churches fail to grow? Ephesians makes it clear. Growth happens as we are joined together with each part doing its own work.

The church has been disabled far too long. Much of it is without legs and arms and with very little heart. Jesus, the head of the church, needs a working and healthy body to complete His mission on Earth. You have a part in the body. You have a function. Will you do it? Will you help His body reach, touch, and move? Will you become a Second Mile Leader?

Bewildered In The Wilderness

The problem that arises when ministry is concentrated around one person is not unique to our day or in the early church. It emerges quickly upon Israel's exit from Egypt. They have one man who is expected to lead them. Moses is their deliverer, their intercessor, and their judge, and he quickly becomes weary in this leadership role.

> *Moses heard all the families standing in the doorways of their tents whining, and the LORD became extremely angry. Moses was also very aggravated. And Moses*

said to the LORD, "Why are you treating me, your servant, so harshly? Have mercy on me! What did I do to deserve the burden of all these people? Did I give birth to them? Did I bring them into the world? Why did you tell me to carry them in my arms like a mother carries a nursing baby? How can I carry them to the land you swore to give their ancestors? Where am I supposed to get meat for all these people? They keep whining to me, saying, 'Give us meat to eat!' **I can't carry all these people by myself! The load is far too heavy! If this is how you intend to treat me, just go ahead and kill me. Do me a favor and spare me this misery!"** *(Numbers 11:10-14 NLT)*

Moses is one of my heroes in the Bible; I cannot imagine being him. He had some serious resolve and grit. He was steady, faithful, and gracious when I would have prayed for God just to wipe everybody out and try again, yet it sounds in this passage as though he is at the edge of walking away. He sounds depressed and despondent. He would rather God kill him than have to continue under his current leadership load.

I read an article recently that described just how many pastors suffer with depression. The numbers are startling. To know that you stand as a leader who oversees people and their eternal destinies carries a tremendous weight of responsibility. To compound the matter, the results of ministry are usually vague and intangible.

**Pastors were never meant to carry
the burden of the church alone.**

When I worked construction, I could stand back at the end of the day and admire what all my hard work had accomplished. Whether it was a paved driveway or a framed house, the results were clear. Ministry results are not so clear. While it is easy to count numbers in a room, cars in the parking lot, and cash in the offering, those are not the goals of ministry. The goal is changed lives. It is often hard, however, to quantify a change in people's attitudes, motives, beliefs, and hearts. Sometimes it's just hard to measure progress.

Perhaps this is what is driving Moses to the end of himself. Yes, God has done amazing miracles. He has made a way through the sea. He is providing supernaturally for the children of Israel, but it never seems to be enough. The people are never happy. They are constantly complaining.

Moses is at his wit's end. He is out of energy and resolve. He has reached a breaking point. He is not asking for God to kill everyone; he is just looking for answers. I can hear him asking questions that I might ask: "Is this the way it really has to be? Is this the way ministry is supposed to look? God, is this the way Your nation, Your chosen people, are supposed to act? What happens when they have even more kids? I don't know if I can make it!" Moses has reached the end of the line of being able to carry the load of ministry. So he asks God for a solution. God provides one.

Then the LORD said to Moses, "Gather before me sev-

*enty men who are recognized as elders and leaders of Israel. Bring them to the Tabernacle to stand there with you. I will come down and talk to you there. I will take some of the Spirit that is upon you, and I will put the Spirit upon them also. **They will bear the burden of the people along with you, so you will not have to carry it alone.** (Numbers 11:16-17 NLT)*

God answers Moses's prayer, not by parting a sea but by providing partners in ministry. God wants Israel to grow and his leader to survive. He never planned for Moses to bear the weight alone. Just like Moses, pastors were never meant to carry the burden of the church alone. He didn't just give one man; He called the *ekklésia*. We are the church. We are the body. Do you know your function? Are you shouldering it or shirking it? Are you a Second Mile Leader who has stepped into the gifting and calling on your life?

Moses was very excited that God would multiply ministry. He was not fearful that people would rise up and walk away from him if God started using other people in the congregation to do ministry. Watch the heart of Moses when new leaders emerge who are able to do at this point what only he had been able to do previously.

So Moses went out and reported the LORD's words to the people. He gathered the seventy elders and stationed them around the Tabernacle. And the LORD came down in the cloud and spoke to Moses. **Then he gave the seventy elders the same Spirit that was upon Moses. And when the Spirit rested upon them, they prophesied.** *But this never happened again. Two men, Eldad and Medad, had stayed behind in the camp. They were listed among the elders, but they had not gone out to the Tabernacle. Yet the Spirit rested upon them as well, so they prophesied there in the camp. A young man ran and reported to Moses, "Eldad and Medad are prophesying in the camp!" Joshua son of Nun, who had been Moses' assistant since his youth, protested, "Moses, my master, make them stop!" But Moses replied,* **"Are you jealous for my sake? I wish that all the LORD's people were prophets and that the LORD would put his Spirit upon them all!"** *(Numbers 11:24-29 NLT)*

Moses wasn't threatened; he was thrilled! He wasn't hoarding ministry. He was looking for help! He was grateful God had gifted people to come alongside and help take care of what needed to be done. He exclaims, "I wish that *all* the Lord's people were prophets!"

I would guess that part of your pastor's prayer to God involves asking that He would put his Spirit on more people in his congregation. He is likely praying for more leaders and laborers. He is probably asking God to send more people that he can empower. He is asking for people to come alongside him so the church can continue to grow. If you will become a Second Mile Leader, you can be the answer to his prayer.

When pastors are able to train leaders and delegate authority, church growth potential is unlimited.

Pastors are looking for people who can lead and love well. They are not looking to keep all the power in their pockets. They are not on an ego trip hoping no one else will have a voice or a vision in the church. They looking for people with potential. Are you that person? Are you willing for the Spirit of the Lord to be placed on you so you can be empowered as well?

The Jethro Principle

Another example of multiplying ministry occurs in Exodus 18. Moses's father-in-law, Jethro, comes to visit. He is amazed at what God is doing in the nation of Israel. He praises God for the work that He has done, but then he sees how Moses is dealing with Israel's problems and is appalled. He offers some leadership coaching and correction to Moses.

Moses' father-in-law, Jethro, the priest of Midian, heard about everything God had done for Moses and his people, the Israelites. He heard especially about how the Lord had rescued them from Egypt. "Praise the Lord," Jethro said, "for he has rescued you from the Egyptians and from Pharaoh. Yes, he has rescued Israel from the powerful hand of Egypt! I know now that the Lord is greater than all other gods, because he rescued his people from the oppression of the proud Egyptians." (Exodus 18:1,10-11 NLT)

Jethro had heard the stories of what God had been doing in this young nation. He had heard of the miracles God had performed. The miraculous works of God caused him to express faith in Him. Yet when he witnessed Moses's methods, he realized the man could use some wise advice.

*The next day, Moses took his seat to hear the people's disputes against each other. They waited before him from morning till evening. **When Moses' father-in-law saw all that Moses was doing for the people, he asked, "What are you really accomplishing here? Why are you trying to do all this alone while everyone stands around you from morning till evening?"** Moses replied, "Because the people come to me to get a ruling from God. When a dispute arises, they come to me, and I am the one who settles the case between the quarreling parties. I inform the people of God's decrees and give them his instructions." **"This is not good!" Moses' father-in-law exclaimed. "You're going to wear yourself out—and the people, too. This job is too heavy a burden for you to handle all by yourself.** Now listen to me, and let me give* *you a word of advice, and may God be with you. You should continue to be the people's representative before God, bringing their disputes to him. Teach them God's decrees, and give them his instructions. Show them how to conduct their lives. But select from all the people some capable, honest men who fear God and hate bribes. Appoint them as leaders over groups of one thousand, one hundred, fifty, and ten. They should always be available to solve the people's common disputes, but have them bring the major cases to you. Let the leaders decide the smaller matters themselves. They will help you carry the load, making the task easier for you. If you follow this advice, and if God commands you to do so, then you will be able to endure the pressures, and all these people will go home in peace." Moses listened to his father-in-law's advice and followed his suggestions. (Exodus 18:13-24 NLT)*

Jethro's two-part interaction is a bit like hearing something incredible happening at a church somewhere else in the country. We go and check it out. At first everything seems good from the outside. Based on the final product, we assume this group really has its act together and we have much to learn from them. When we get to peek behind the curtain and see the inner workings, however, we think, "Really? How is something this disorganized and dysfunctional capable of seeing incredible things like that happen?"

Jethro had heard the stories, but now he saw the systems. He was taken aback by the lack of structure associated with such a great move of God. He offered Moses some very wise advise: Train leaders. Teach other people how to do what you do. Delegate authority. Let them deal with the majority of the small matters and you will be needed only when they cannot figure it out for themselves.

This principle still works today, and it is how the church is really able to grow. When pastors are able to train leaders and delegate authority to a group of believers that understand they are the *ekklésia*, the church growth potential is unlimited.

The problem Moses faced to this point was the same problem your pastor likely faces. People considered him the elevated leader. He was the person who spoke directly to God. Every single person wanted to get his decisions directly from Moses. Sound familiar? This seems very much like a church built around a professional clergy. People want time with the pastor. They want him to come to their house, take them to dinner, attend their kids' events, and do everything with them and for them. When the church continues in this mind-set though, growth is stifled. God never intended for this to happen. He wants your pastor to be able to train you to become a Second Mile Leader so together you can accomplish the vision God has for your church and your city.

As long as there are people who are unreached, destined for Heaven or Hell, growth is not an option.

Ready For Revival

God is ready to send real revival–exponential growth–the kind that reshapes your city. After all, the Bible tells us that He's not willing that any should perish but all come to repentance. The problem with revival is not God. The problem is the church. We are not ready to receive what God wants to do. We have restricted revival with our system of expecting one man to carry all the wisdom, knowledge, and weight of ministry. Whatever our reason for structuring the church this way, it will never be able to have the type of rapid growth God desires to send until every person does his part and until many people decide they are willing to become the type of leaders who will go the second mile.

Right in the middle of deliverance, Israel was crushing their leader. Right in the middle of revolution, the early church began to face problems that would slow its progress to a crawl. God gave them a solution–appoint leaders. Empower them to do the work.

In the modern church, we have stopped empowering leaders to this level and placed the emphasis on the pastor. We continue to put all our eggs in one basket, and the results are startling! According to Barna Group research, the average size of a church in the Unitred States is 89 adults, 60 percent of churches have less that 100 in attendance, and only 2 percent ever break the 1000 mark.[11] Why might this be? When the ministry is limited to a single individual, the pastor, the capacity of the church is limited to the capacity of the pastor. Any person can effectively lead only a small number of people.

Robin Dunbar, an anthropologist and psychologist, did

extensive research with theories related to our relational capacity. He investigated the number of people we will typically have in our network of friendships and theorized that the average person can effectively maintain relationships with about 150 people. This popularized theory was based on the size of our brain. According to Dunbar, the number can be higher or lower based on our social capacity and networks. When we couple Dunbar's number with Barna's research, it is astounding to see that the average size church in America is less than 100!

So how big do you think your church should be? How many people in your town or city are you interested in seeing come to know Jesus? I can almost guarantee you that your pastor is dissatisfied with the size of your congregation. His desire has nothing to do with his ego or a need to build a name for himself. He is wanting to expand the family of God. We have to get serious about growing the church. Eternal destinies are at stake. As long as there are people who are unreached, destined for Heaven or Hell, growth is not an option.

Carey Nieuwhof, a pastor and church leader in Canada who does much research on church growth and lack of growth, lists several reasons why churches stay small. The top four are that the pastor is the primary caregiver, the leader lacks a strategy, true leaders aren't leading, and volunteers are under-empowered.[12] Isn't this exactly what we've seen in this chapter? Ministry cannot be centered around one person. A system of empowerment and accountability must be in place for our churches to grow.

Your pastor is perfectly capable of leading your church to

be the size it is right now, but what would happen if you became a Second Mile Leader? What would happen if you took on the responsibility and the calling for which God created you? How many people could your church reach?

Your pastor is looking for people who will carry the fire and burning desire of his vision to reach people in your community. He will share his vision with you if you ask. He will empower you to take the call God has on your church and make a portion of it your own. The question is this:

WILL YOU MULTIPLY MINISTRY?

6

RENTERS
VERSUS
OWNERS

"I must do something" always solves
more problems than "Something must be done."
~Author Unknown

For some reason I can never just leave well enough alone. My spiritual gift is change. I love taking a system or structure that is working and find a way to make it better. I do this pretty much everywhere I work and everywhere I live. It's the latter that gets me in the most trouble.

My wife Aimee, like most women, loves to nest. A house is not a home until pictures are placed on walls, furniture is arranged, familiar blankets and pillows are placed, and items are arranged to make her feel that she's in familiar surroundings.

In 2005 we purchased the nicest home we had ever owned. It was a stretch and a struggle. The process of buying it was gut-wrenching. We were near the edge of our budget. The story on whether we were going to be able to make the purchase kept changing. The banks had repossessed the property from the previous owners, so lawyers were involved. One day we would be told that everything was good and we would be able to close on the house soon. The next day everything would change. Finally we were able to close on our dream house. It was amazing–more than we had ever dreamed. We were so elated to be in it; we were thrilled to call it home, and I did nothing for a couple of years. Then one day...

One day I got this crazy idea. What if we completely remodeled the living area of the house? The main living area had a double rock and brick fireplace that separated a formal living room from a family den. They were both a bit cramped. I had this great idea that if we removed both of these fireplaces, we could join these two small rooms together into a large open living area. It seemed like a good idea. Oh, I almost forgot to say that my idea was to do all this while remaining in the house.

I was able to talk my wife into how amazing the house would be after these changes, and we proceeded to destroy our home. Electrical wiring hung from the ceiling. Our children were not allowed to enter the living room area without wearing shoes for fear of stepping on a nail. Never mind the risk of electric shock; we certainly didn't want them to get tetanus also.

This remodel took several months and finally was complete. We had installed beautiful hardwood floors and new lighting and had created an open floor plan by joining the two rooms. My wife nested again. It was home. She forgave me. It *was* better. Just as I promised. This was a perfect situation. Then one day...

One day I came home and began to talk to my wife about the possibility of moving into a home a few miles outside the city. Doing this would allow our oldest daughter to have the horse she had always dreamed of. We could just walk outside and be with the animals in nature, plant a garden, have a pool, and even go hunting.

You guessed it. She's amazing. After minimal amounts of begging, pleading, and negotiating, she said it would be fine. We could move and do this. So we left our nice newly remodeled home and moved into a small country house.

In order to move into this house in the country, we rented our updated and remodeled home. Everything was great. We cut our living expenses, paid off debt, and had a stream of income from our home in town. My daughter loved having her horse right outside. My son and I hunted a lot. We loved it. It was home. Things were awesome! Then one day…

One day I had a conversation with Pastor Don Nordin about the possibility of our family moving to Texas to be on their team and pastor alongside them. We talked it over, prayed about it, and decided this was our next step in God's plan for our lives.

In order to move to Texas, we first needed to move back into our home in town to get it ready to sell. Now if you've never had the privilege of owning rental property, I'll let you in on a little secret: Renters don't care for a house the same way the owners do.

It was nice to have a stream of income while it was rented and we were living in the country house. Our living expenses had been half what they were previously. We were in pretty good shape financially. That was great. We were going to need the wiggle room in the budget.

We moved back into the house February 1, 2015, and I had to be in Houston, Texas, by February 28. We thought it best to move in to fix up the house and stage it in order to get the best price possible for our home.

The renters had NOT cared for it as we did as owners. What we had sweat to make look nice they had damaged with indifference. It had been in terrific condition when we moved to the country. It was a bit overwhelming to see our home needing so many things retouched, repainted, and repaired. We worked *extremely* hard to get the house in condition to sell for the amount we needed in order to purchase a home in Houston, Texas. We worked every single day. In fact, the day I moved to Houston there was still work to be done. My family stayed behind to finish the repairs in order to show and sell the house.

The day I left town I was showing my son, Hunter, how to do some work and nearly sliced off my finger in the process. When I piled into my car with my youngest daughter, Kyndra, and drove out on that snowy February morning I was exhausted physically, mentally, and emotionally, and my finger was throbbing–a reminder that renters don't care as much as owners.

Renters are problem *finders*. Owners are problem *fixers*.

Renters Versus Owners

See, renters have **_rights_**. They expect you to come and fix the air conditioner when it does not work. They want you to fix the roof if it leaks. They expect you to come and fix the garage door opener, the dishwasher, the stove, and the sink if it is clogged or leaking. It's not *their* problem! They are the renters. They are entitled to have everything they pay for in working condition.

The owners, however, have **_responsibilities_**. They have no one else coming to fix the problems. It falls on their shoulders. They have to pay for the repairs or do the repairs themselves. All the problems roll uphill. They realize "the buck stops here." More accurately, the bucks don't stop here. They flow into your checkbook and right back out as you pay for everything that is broken.

Renters are problem *finders*. Owners are problem *fixers*. When renters discover a functional issue in the property, they pick up the phone and inform the owner, "You need to come and fix this." They take zero responsibility for the problem. They rightfully expect the owner to come and address the issue, and ultimately, if the owner leaves the problem unattended, the renter will simply find another owner to rent from.

Good property owners typically respond quickly to complaints and issues. They know it's really in their best interest to keep the renter happy. Truthfully it needs to be this way. It's only fair to the renter. One part of their contractual expectations is that if they give you money for something in working order, that item should be kept in working order.

Many Christians bring a renter's mentality to the church. They believe they are paying the pastor to keep everything in working order. It's his job to fix problems. But this was never the intention of God regarding how the church is to function. We are *all* owners of the mission of Jesus Christ.

Are you renting or owning the vision of your church? It is fairly easy to tell. When you hear of a problem that needs to be addressed, what is your first reaction? Is it to try to fix the problem or to inform someone whom you consider to be the responsible party? Are you a problem finder or a problem fixer?

In a previous chapter we told the story of Everybody, Somebody, Anybody, and Nobody. Are you an anybody who could but you think somebody else should? When you own the vision, the ministry, the property, you know there is no one else to pass it off to. It is your responsibility to address the situation. Sure, you wish it was not your problem to deal with. Sure, you wish you could just bury your head in the sand, but you know that you cannot in good conscience avoid the issue. It is your problem to solve.

The home we purchased in Texas is a two-story home. One side of the house is away from the sun and is constantly damp. It continues to accumulate mildew and needs powerwashing at least once each year. It is really high and a bit intimidating. I do not want to deal with or fix it. Part of me wants to ignore the situation and hope it will simply go away, but I know that if I don't deal with the issue a nice letter from our homeowner's association is going to inform me that everyone in my neighborhood thinks my house looks ugly.

It would be absurd to think that my next door neighbor will take a weekend and powerwash my house. Worse yet, our relationship would probably deteriorate if I knocked on his door and told him I expected him to deal with my problem and issue. Yet this is exactly how we treat the church. Problems that we should address personally and deal with are passed off to someone who is not even associated with the problem or the person. We do this because we have the mentality of a renter. We think that the problems are not ours and that we are entitled to have them fixed on our behalf.

We think to ourselves, "Someone should come and deal with this situation." Yes, they should. You should. I should. And if we own the vision of the church and the Great Commission, we will.

When your church has an outreach or a project, do you show up? Better yet, do you show up early and stay late? Are you supporting the ministry of your church by giving, attending, and serving? Are you consuming when you should be contributing? Are you a problem finder or a problem fixer?

If you have not caught the vision of your pastor or leaders, do you ask questions, seeking to understand the heart and purpose behind the activities of your church so you can catch the vision? Do you position yourself in conversations that will allow you to grab hold of the heart of your leaders and run with what God has placed in their hearts? Or do you show up only on the weekend ready to be served spiritual bread but leave as soon as possible, allowing others to clean up after the meal you just consumed?

If you realize at this point that your mentality is more of a renter than an owner and you would like to move to ownership of the mission of your local church, there are some things you can do that will help shift your viewpoint and move your mentality to one of an owner.

Ask To Hear The Leader's Vision

I remember the first time I was able to hear the vision of my Pastor, Larry Pyle. He had moved to Arkansas from California. The church he returned to pastor was stagnant. The congregation was content to have church as usual and do the same thing over and over, ignoring those literally just outside the church walls. Our parking lot was full of teenagers every Friday and Saturday night, and he began to reach them by putting on concerts and working to draw them in.

People in the church were unhappy with the disruption of the status quo. They felt the teenagers and people we were reaching would destroy the paint and the carpet and would damage the facility. Pastor Larry poured out his vision and shared why he felt this was the right thing to do–to go after the lost. Seems like a no-brainer, right? Apparently not. Many people rose up in the church in opposition to him.

As he poured out his vision for our church, I decided I would own that vision. You must hear the vision to see if you can align with it. If you're in the wrong church with the wrong vision, you need to find one where you are in alignment with the pastor's heart and vision.

Ask The Leaders What They See

If you are struggling to understand programming and structure, ask for a meeting with the leader of your department or your church; it is okay to ask questions for understanding. Most people avoid asking questions to understand and delay conversation until their frustration is so high that the questions they ask are not to understand but undermine. Typically they do this in public settings and cause discord and division within the church. Team members who were previously in full support of the vision and direction now begin to question the vision as well.

Most leaders are transparent and willing to answer questions. In many cases they are willing to adjust their approach, programming, or methodology. They may indeed need your fresh eyes to see something that they are missing, but even though you may think your perspective is the right one, approach these conversations in humility. Make sure your motives are to understand, not to undermine.

My youth pastor, Thomas Hale, told us a story about a job he had at a golf course. His boss took him out one day and showed him the driving range and asked Thomas what he saw. Thomas said he saw a driving range. His boss said, "I see uncollected golf balls that I can't put in buckets and sell. I'm losing money while they sit out there." He then told Thomas, "I don't want to have to tell you this again. If you can't see what I see, I don't need you."

Is that true of you and me? Are we blind to what needs to be done in order to accomplish the mission, purpose, and vision of the church?

Jesus said to his disciples, "I tell you, open your eyes and look at the fields! They are ripe for harvest" (John 4:35 NIV). Jesus saw something they couldn't see. What was the solution? **Look**!

Is the problem we have that we can't see or that we simply won't look? Are we avoiding responsibility by keeping our eyes closed and burying our head in the sand? If so, we are acting like renters, not owners. Ask to see what your leader sees.

**We need to stop being armor-bearers
and start being vision carriers.**

Verbally Commit To The Vision

Proverbs says, *"The tongue has the power of life and death"
(Proverbs 18:21, NIV).* Knowing this, we have to verbalize our commitment to our pastors, shepherds, and leaders. We have to choose our commitment and then speak it aloud to them.

I did this in 1989 when I walked up to Pastor Larry Pyle at a business meeting and told him I was with him. When I spoke those words out loud, something happened in my heart. From that point forward, I was bound to that man's vision. I left two different times to go and serve on staff with other churches, yet I never made the same commitments to those pastors that I did to Larry Pyle in Arkansas. For that reason, I only lasted about a year in each of those ministries. Both times I desired strongly to move back to his church and serve his vision. Why? Because I was bound to that vision with my commitment I had made to him. I chose his vision, so I was never comfortable anywhere else.

In 2015 we were interviewing for a campus pastor position at CT Church in Houston, Texas. In one of the interviews, a church boardmember asked about how my family and I were going to be able to make this move since it was uprooting us from all we had known for so long. I hadn't prepped for this question, so I really didn't know what to say. I said the first thing that came to my mind.

I said, "I guess I'll just say like Ruth said to Naomi, 'Your people will be my people, and your God will be my God.'"

The moment I made the statement, it took my breath away. My eyes welled up with tears. My wife felt the same thing happen in her. There was a spiritual shift—a new vow and a new verbal commitment. We had said to another pastor that we would stand with him and share his heart, vision, and dream.

The move from rural Arkansas to Houston was significant. Pretty much everything about this place is different. People are people, but the landscape, the culture, the amount of people...Dear Lord, all the people! It is so different. There are no hills. There are few trees. We live next to the ship channel, which is pretty ugly. And yet it is beautiful here because the people and the vision we have chosen are here.

Your confession makes all the difference. People wonder why they can't own the vision, and the whole time they are finding problems and complaining. You cannot bless and curse at the same time.

Have you made your commitment to the vision known? It's not for your pastor. It's for you. It's so you can become an owner, not a renter. A transfer of heart, passion, and desire will happen. You won't see the same anymore. You'll have the eyes that can see the harvest.

**There is a difference between a life that's filled full
and a life that's fulfilled.**

Serve The Vision

In order to own the vision, you have to serve it. You have to be willing to arrange your schedule to participate. We have so many people at our church who work very strenuous work schedules yet still lead life groups, participate in outreaches, and lead teams on the weekends. They are the real heros and ministers in our church. Without them being owners, we could not do what we do.

In the past people have asked to be my armor-bearer. I know they mean well, but I honestly don't need someone to carry my personal belongings from my seat in the auditorium to the trunk of my car. What I really need is for someone to carry my vision, and that is exactly what your pastor needs, too! He may allow you to "honor" him by calling him pastor, designating him a parking spot, or starting his car and bringing it around to the front. Those are nice gestures of honor. But I'd be willing to place a bet that if he had to trade those things that "honor" him for people that actually follow the vision that God has placed in his heart, he'd make the trade in a skinny minute. We need to stop just trying to honor our pastors by preferential treatment and titles. We need to serve the vision God has placed in their heart. We need to stop being armor-bearers and start being vision carriers.

When I felt that God was wanting me to serve the vision of Larry Pyle in Arkansas, I rearranged my work schedule. I told my boss that I couldn't work certain shifts that would take me out of ministry. I chose to make less money and work harder jobs just so I could make myself available and maximize my participation in ministry.

I cannot tell you what this looks like for you. That's a conversation between you and Jesus, and it is one He wants to have. I can tell you this—without those conversations your schedule will be full. You get to choose what occupies your time. No matter what you are doing to fill your life, remember this: There is a difference between a life that's filled full and a life that's fulfilled.

You have a purpose. You're the only one who can fulfill it, and you will never be happier than when you do what God created you to do. Yes, it may cost you. You may have to shift or shelve some dreams and desires, but the payoff will be a "well done, good and faithful servant" when you stand before Jesus. Live for that moment.

If you can see the impact, you will be willing to serve even when it's outside your preferences.

Look For the Impact Of The Vision

Regardless of whether or not you completely buy in to the vision of the house, you're always going to have issues with part of it. That is normal. We are human. Because none of us are exactly alike, no two of us have the same preferences. Your leadership will do things in a way that isn't the way you would do it if you were in charge.

When we first moved to this church, several things were done differently from the way we did them at my previous church. Some were minor, so I could overlook them. Others really bothered me. What I had to do was look past my preferences and see the purpose.

One particular ministry I didn't care for because of the way it was presented and packaged. I struggled with it. Then I heard the testimonies of the impact. I heard of a pastor whose ministry was saved as a result of what we were doing. They were in a desperate season in their ministry. In fact they were ready to return home and resign their position. It was in this lowest of moments that they received from this ministry we were doing. They were not only encouraged to continue in their difficult season but also to surrender completely their *own* preferences for the call God had put on their life. This humbled me and changed my perspective. Their story became my "why."

If you can see the impact, you will be willing to serve even when it's outside your preferences. After all, if you were leading the ministry exactly as you wanted, there would be people who wouldn't like everything about the way *you* do it either. So embrace the tension. Serve anyway. See the impact of changed lives and be grateful for the honor to be a part.

**When we allow feelings to determine our decisions,
we rob ourselves of our destiny.**

Act Your Way Into Feeling

Many of us wait until we "feel like it" to engage in activities that are very beneficial. This is true of me and the gym. I keep waiting to go and work out until I feel like going to work out. I know I will be happy once I go. I will be proud of myself. But guess what? I have not gone for a while because the feeling comes *after* the doing.

I heard this quotation somewhere in the past: "Unsuccessful people feel their way into acting. Successful people act their way into feeling." That is the big secret. When we allow the feelings to determine our action, we will live with inaction. All of us are tired and afraid and suffer with discouragement. When we allow feelings to determine our decisions, we rob ourselves of our destiny. Think of it. If we went to work only when we felt like it, most of us would be jobless and homeless. We have to do things when we don't feel like doing them until we do feel like doing them.

When we step into the vision that God has for the house that we serve, we probably will not feel like it. Many days we will wish we could just let someone else take care of the problem. We would like to pass the buck. There may be days when we desire to be "just a regular church attender." We will not want to be Second Mile Leaders. We will not want to be owners. We want just to rent for a while.

Renters say, "That sounds crazy; I'm not doing it."
Owners say, "That sounds crazy; let's do it!"

Let me challenge you to go "all in" for the vision of your church for 1 year. Have a pre-decided "yes." Decide that you will do what you're asked for 12 months–that if it is possible, you will have a whatever, whenever, wherever attitude. At the end of the 12 months, just see if you are not a completely different person–one who is a Second Mile Leader.

You will find yourself an owner, not a renter.

> *One day Jonathan said to his armor bearer, "Come on, let's go over to where the Philistines have their outpost." But Jonathan did not tell his father what he was doing. "Let's go across to the outpost of those pagans," Jonathan said to his armor bearer. "Perhaps the LORD will help us, for nothing can hinder the LORD. He can win a battle whether he has many warriors or only a few!"* **"Do what you think is best," the armor bearer replied. "I'm with you completely, whatever you decide."** *"All right then," Jonathan told him. "We will cross over and let them see us. If they say to us, 'Stay where you are or we'll kill you,' then we will stop and not go up to them. But if they say, 'Come on up and fight,' then we will go up. That will be the LORD's sign that he will help us defeat them." (1 Samuel 14:1,6-10 NLT)*

I know very little about war. I have never served in the military, but I have to tell you my opinion of this battle strategy: It's stupid. Perhaps it is one of the stupidest I have ever heard. First they give away the element of surprise by revealing themselves to the enemy; then they allow the enemy's words to determine their response. I have to tell you that if I had been Jonathan's armor-bearer, I would have let him do this one alone. I would wonder if he had been out in the sun a little too long that day. It seems that Jonathan had a bit of a mental problem.

That is not what the armor-bearer did, however. Instead he made a verbal commitment to Jonathan. He said, "Do what you think is best. I'm with you completely, whatever you decide." Wow! Jonathan's armor-bearer carried more than just armor. He carried the vision. He went into battle, willing to risk his own life to accomplish what Jonathan thought was a good plan even if he might have thought it was a bad strategy.

The armor-bearer's words give us a clue to what we might hear a real owner of the vision say. Notice this: Renters say, "That sounds crazy; I'm not doing it." Owners say, "That sounds crazy; let's do it!"

Your pastor may be brilliant, but chances are he is not the smartest person ever to live. He does not have all the answers, but God has anointed him to lead your church. He has a vision to do something about the evil that Hell is perpetrating on your city. Your pastor is not asking you to follow him because he has it all figured out. He is asking you to help him figure it out as you serve the vision God has for your local church. Your pastor is looking for people who will follow and implement a vision no matter the risk or the cost–whatever the sacrifice, the position, job, or strategy, he's looking for people who will say this:

"DO WHAT YOU THINK IS BEST. I'M WITH YOU COMPLETELY, WHATEVER YOU DECIDE."

7

CIRCLES ARE BETTER THAN ROWS

You grow bigger by thinking smaller.

- Pastor Kemp Holden

A few years ago a friend and I were riding bikes on some trails in our city. We had ridden for a few miles and made the entire circuit back to where we started. He asked me if I felt like going around again. It felt great riding the trails in the woods. It was awesome having the wind blow in my face as we rode along looking at nature and exercising. Everything in me wanted to say yes to another circuit. Except my right knee. There was a hint of pain in it. Being a person who has been in athletics for many years, I simply shrugged off the pain and said, "Yeah, let's do it!"

That decision was a mistake. My knee had been slightly injured on the first trip around the circuit, and with each pump of the pedal I was damaging the cartilage inside it. When we finished the second circuit, my knee was in a lot of pain. I was pedaling a lot less efficiently. My left leg was ready to push hard, but my right leg was fairly useless.

I was riding the bike, but very inefficiently. Bicycles are designed to be ridden with force exerted equally on each pedal. While you are powering the bike with the force of your stroke with one leg, the second pedal is returning into position so it can be pushed down with the other leg. It is a coordinated effort requiring two pedals and two working legs. I started out with two working legs and finished with only one. What began as a day to exercise and enjoy the outdoors ended with knee surgery and some time for recovery indoors.

A One-Pedal Church

The church that we inherited from Constantine functions much like a bicycle that's missing a pedal. It is largely powered by one type of meeting where the entire church gathers in a single room to listen to a single individual whose talent is showcased every week.

This assembly of the congregation is designed to be a monologue. One communicator gives one idea. It would be chaos to have 100 to 10,000 people who are assembled in the room attempt a dialogue with the person on the stage. Two-way communication would descend rapidly into confusion. Everyone would leave with no new understanding, revelation, or clear next steps. So instead, the congregation listens politely and passively as the pastor gives them their latest revelation of God's word.

If all goes well in this meeting, some of the people come to the front or raise their hands in their seats affirming they are making a commitment to the topic at hand. "Yes," they are saying by their presence in the altar or by the lifting of their hand, "we agree that we need to address this issue in our lives. We commit to the change."

Offering buckets are passed, tithes and offerings are given, the worship team leads us in song, and people leave.

Upon leaving the service, "real life" hits the congregation– bills to pay, schedules to keep, homes to clean, deadlines to meet. The remainder of the week is spent focusing on "real-world" problems– the issues that are really pressing in their homes and their lives. As much as they were stirred Sunday morning, the connection between the Sunday sermon and the Monday mundane never happens. With their focus on real life, the sermon fades. It seems so distant, so irrelevant. They think, "What was it the pastor talked about again?" It is so hard to remember in the hustle and bustle of life, yet something nagging in the back of our minds causes us to think the sermon is supposed to matter for more than just Sunday. It is supposed to apply to Monday through Saturday. But how?

Churches that focus only on the weekend services are like riding a bicycle with only one pedal. It can be done, but it will require twice the effort and produce half the return. One leg will grow massively while the other will atrophy.

This is exactly what has happened with the adoption of the Constantinian model of the church. We have lost half of the way the church was designed to function. The weekend service has become the sole activity for most people who participate in church at all. With the focus solely on large group gatherings, churches draw large crowds but produce few disciples.

Jesus did not send us to make converts.
He sent us to make disciples.

The Pattern Of The Early Church

The New Testament church followed a different pattern. They gathered in two different types of meetings. Acts 2:46 says, "They worshiped **together at the Temple** each day, **met in homes for the Lord's Supper**, and shared their meals with great joy and generosity."

The pattern of the early church was a collective gathering at the temple or some other public space, followed by a meeting in a smaller setting in homes. There they shared the Lord's supper with one another. Communion was not experienced as a pre-packaged wafer and cup. It was an actual meal they shared in homes.

> *You know that I have not hesitated to preach anything that would be helpful to you but have taught you **publicly <u>and</u>** from **house to house**. (Acts 20:20 NIV)*

Again we see the pattern repeated. Paul says they had two meeting types: the public (collective or corporate) gathering followed by the second gathering in the house.

When we realize that many of the church's meetings were conducted in smaller settings, things in scripture become clearer and make more sense. Paul, for example, gives commands in 1 Corinthians 14 on how to conduct our meetings:

> *"What then, brothers? When you come together, **<u>each one</u> has a hymn, a lesson, a revelation, a tongue, or an interpretation**.*

Let all things be done for building up."
(1 Corinthians 14:26 ESV)

Paul says that in this type of gathering *every single person* should participate. Each should contribute a hymn, a teaching, a revelation, a tongue, or an interpretation. Imagine obeying this command in each weekend service! If 200 adults are in your auditorium, you're talking about 200 speakers! If you think your pastor preaches a long time, just give 200 people a microphone and see what happens! Few of us would remain to the end of a service like that; even fewer would return to risk a second visit.

If none of us want to go to a church that follows the pattern of Paul's instruction, how then are we to be Biblically obedient to the structure he has for New Testament worship? This type of meeting is one in a smaller setting, in a home. The reason we miss this is because of the way we think of "going to church." In this passage about the conduct of gatherings, when Paul uses the word "church" we immediately have a picture of what that means. We are conditioned to think of the church as the building or "going to church" as the weekend service, but the New Testament church met in large gatherings and in smaller more intimate gatherings in homes. So while we are thinking of church as the weekend service, in this passage Paul is addressing a smaller more intimate gathering of believers that meets in a *house*.

In a home setting with just a few people gathered together, everyone can contribute. Instead of a monologue, there can be dialogue. In this setting, multiple people share out of the abundance that God is revealing to each of them. There can be encouragement, accountability, and support.

Many of us miss this as we read the scriptures. We are so conditioned to "go to church" and passively participate that we are missing an enormous part of what Christian living and community are all about. The rhythm of church life includes listening to learn on the weekend and active engagement in groups in homes. The early church did both:

> And every day, **_in the temple_** and from **_house_** to **_house_**, they did not cease teaching and preaching Jesus as the Christ. (Acts 5:42 ESV)

> Greet Priscilla and Aquila, my fellow workers in Christ Jesus. They risked their lives for me. Not only I but all the churches of the Gentiles are grateful to them. Greet also the church that meets at their **_house_**. (Romans 16:3-5 NIV)

> Give my greetings to the brothers at Laodicea, and to Nympha and the church in her **_house_**.
> (Colossians 4:15 ESV)

> And Apphia our sister and Archippus our fellow soldier, and the church in your **_house_**. (Philemon 1:2 ESV)

The early church had a pattern of meeting publicly, but it

also met in homes. I believe this is the missing pedal from the bicycle in many of our churches. We are content to gather on the weekend and return to our homes with little or no difference made in our lives. This is an underpowered and ineffective church.

Disciples cannot be manufactured simply by liturgy. They must be molded through sharing life.

Make Disciples, Not Christians

This matters so much to me because I am not interested in making Christians. I am determined to make disciples. We have many people who claim the title of "Christian" in our nation who bear no signs of following Jesus other than a catchy culturally cool title, a fish symbol bumper sticker, or a cross hanging around their neck.

I am not interested in simply having more people claim the *title* of Christian. What I desire to see is people who fulfill the responsibilities of a disciple–a follower of Jesus who is working to become fully obedient to all the commands of Christ. Jesus did not send us to make converts. He sent us to make disciples.

Disciples cannot be manufactured simply by liturgy. They must be molded through sharing life. They cannot be fully formed by hearing a Sunday sermon and singing songs. This is helpful, but it is not complete. Something else is required–life-on-life relationship. Sharing. Accountability.

On Sundays we gather and sit in rows. We are seated beside

someone. We look around and over someone. We sit quietly as some-one else speaks. It is not that Sundays are ineffective; they are simply incomplete. These gatherings serve as a catalyst for forward move-ment. They are the push to get us moving. If we really want to make disciples, however, it takes relationship. For relationship, circles are better than rows.

As a preacher, teacher, and communicator, I spend hours working on what I plan to say and how I will say it. I work hard to turn phrases, find illustrations, and create memorable sayings in an effort not only to get my point across but also to make it stick until it can make a difference. I listen to many podcasts to learn better ways to communicate effectively. I want people to leave the service and have a thought stuck in their heads. I hope to propel them to life change long after the emotion and experience of the service are over.

All of the effort to create this (hopefully) memorable mes-sage–praying, researching, writing, editing, practicing–is delivered and gone in about 30 minutes on a Sunday morning. Once the ser-mon and service are over, I am left with many nagging questions: They heard the Word, but did they understand it? Did God speak to them? Were they even listening? Did they pray a prayer of com-mitment? Did they make a promise to change? By the middle of the week, will they recall the revelation God gave them? Will it matter anymore? Will they follow through after the emotion is gone and real life takes over? Do they have anyone in their life they will ask to hold them accountable?

I am nagged by these thoughts as people leave and our park-ing lot empties. I am not narcissistic, hoping for affirmation. My desire is to see all of us (including myself) hear and obey the word. Hebrews 3:15 cautions, *"Today, if you hear his voice, do not harden your hearts."* My concern is that the more we hear God's word and fail to obey it, we simply harden our hearts to Him. I do not want to be part of a system that causes people to become less like Christ while thinking they look and act just like Him.

More questions come: Is each Sunday actually making it *more* difficult for them to become a disciple? Are they deceiving themselves into thinking they are great disciples because they hear the word yet don't do what it says as James 1:22 says? Am I helping them *think* they are good Christians when all the while they are terrible disciples? Do they latch on to the word, only to have it snatched away by the enemy? Are the cares of life choking out their commitments to God as they intend to follow through but real life crowds out the word that's planted in their hearts?

See, I'm not about just getting a group of people together in a room to hear me preach. I want to see people give themselves fully to God. I receive a much greater thrill seeing people take their next steps as believers than I do seeing them raise their hands for salvation. I'm more interested in Him being their Lord, not just their Savior.

This happens in our churches every single week. Sunday morning plants a seed. It's a catalyst, a spark. Without attention, however, that spark goes out. What could have been a raging fire is now extinguished, and we wait again until Sunday morning to see if we can get the fire lit once more.

Try this for an example exercise. Tell me the points from

your pastor's message this Sunday. What changed in your life at the end of the service? How are you different today because of the decision you made? The likelihood that you enjoyed the service is high; otherwise, you're probably already on the hunt for another church to attend. Even if you enjoyed it, what is different in your life because you were there?

In the New Testament church, they met not only in public settings but also in homes. There they emphasized worship; practice of spiritual gifts; teaching; prayer; fellowship; evangelism; the Lord's Supper; baptism; and the care of widows, orphans, and the poor.

There was personal interaction of each one because they were small enough in number that every person had the opportunity to contribute to the meeting as described in 1 Corinthians 14.

The meeting in homes of the New Testament resembles our small group ministries of today. The small group context was central to the growth of disciples and rapid expansion of the church.

In a small group setting not only can every believer participate, every believer can receive many elements not available in the corporate setting. As each believer participates, personal growth as a disciple happens more rapidly than passive attendance and listening on the weekend.

**Sharing our ideas and convictions
motivates us to model them in our lives.**

Participation

Instead of coming and sitting quietly and politely, believers gathered in small groups have the opportunity to contribute to the group and exercise their spiritual gifts. If they have a revelation, they can share it. If they are a good singer, they can lead in a song. If they have a spiritual gift, they can contribute it. If they have insight into God's word, they can give it.

Participation is key to the growth of a disciple. As we verbalize ideas, they are clarified and solidified in our minds. If we are responsible to teach or communicate ideas we have learned, we tend to pay closer attention. If we study a topic to present it, our understanding deepens substantially. Sharing our ideas and convictions motivates us to model them in our lives. The small group environment combines all these elements and factors, causing much more rapid growth in a disciple.

Care

Many people look to their church office to take care of their needs. If they have a financial need, they stop by the building to request benevolence. If they are hospitalized, they call the office to make sure the pastor comes to visit. This causes a twofold problem.

First, people receive less than optimal care. As the burden of what is supposed to happen naturally through organic relationships is placed back on a professional relationship, people are left to face their problems with little emotional, physical, and financial support.

The pastor should visit when and where he can. He should care for the needs of his flock, yet the needs can never be fully met through a single individual. They were intended to be met through the relationships that make up the church body.

In Galatians Paul writes, *"Bear one another's burdens, and so fulfill the law of Christ (Galatians 6:2 ESV)."* Care is best expressed through tight-knit relationships. People need close friends and family in times of crisis. The members of their small group make up that family. They are able to stand with them through their pain and ordeal.

If the expectation is left on the pastor to do this, many needs in the congregation will go unmet. As frustration rises in the congregation, pressure mounts on the pastor to do more and more, which results in the second part of the two-fold problem. The pastor, unable to meet the demands of a growing congregation, is forced to choose between serving the needs of the church he oversees or his own wife and kids.

Most church people with a pastor-only mind-set assume that because this is his profession the main leader should be there for every single birthday, graduation, and event in their lives. This isn't simply selfishness on the part of the church member; it is ignorance. It's part of the model that was instituted by Constantine. Once relegated to professional clergy, ministry was allowed to be performed only by those duly sanctioned by the state church. Although you won't find many pastors demanding to be the only one allowed to do ministry, this mentality still overshadows many church members. When it comes to prayer, concern, and care, they want it to come from the professional–the pastor. This idea can be changed only as pastors restore the original design of the church and remind their congregations that they expect them to care for one another in small groups, just as in the early church.

If we can recognize that God has made us all kings and priests and that we are all ministers, then we cannot only allow but expect our small group leader or another small group member to pray and care for us. And honestly, that is who we really want in a crisis–someone who is near us, someone with whom we've shared our lives, and someone who will now share theirs with us.

Belonging

The language of the New Testament centers around Biblical community or family. Many times Paul calls those in the church his brothers and sisters. Church was intended to be family. To be family means we have to be together and experience life together. These experiences foster a sense of identity and belonging.

My family loves to watch movies together. If all we did was watch movies, there wouldn't be much depth to our relationship. After the movie is over, however, we talk about it and laugh about it. Thankfully watching movies is not the only thing we do. We take trips together and eat meals together. The things that make us family are the conversation, the community, the care, and the belonging. This "sameness" or identity is what gives us a sense that we belong.

Sadly many of us are experiencing the church like attending a movie. We gather on the weekend, sit side-by-side staring at a speaker, and then leave for home. We then wonder why we feel like we don't belong.

I've often had people tell me they changed churches because they did not feel like they belonged; they say they did not feel connected. I usually ask if they were serving on a team or attending a small group. The answer is typically no. They say they just never got around to it. They place all the responsibility on the church and make zero effort to connect. The truth is that our feeling of connectedness has very little to do with the size of the crowd; it has to do with who we are connected to *in* that crowd.

A church can grow infinitely large if it is comprised of small groups.

If you've ever been invited to someone's home to a party where you knew no one, you probably felt awkward when you showed up. You might have felt conspicuous. Your first action was probably to look for someone you knew so you no longer felt out of place.

Yet in contrast, if you attend an event of thousands, such as a concert, in the company of one or two friends, you feel completely comfortable. Why? Because you are connected. Belonging is not about the size of the crowd; it is about being connected to someone in the crowd.

Belonging requires something beyond the weekend service. It requires conversations in which you discover that person who also likes the things you like. You find a person in the same season of life. You discover someone who's been through what you're experiencing now. You have those "me too" moments. Connections deepen. Relationships are formed. These conversations typically do not happen at the weekend service. It is what happens *between* experiences that deepens the relationship and develops the sense of belonging.

The more experiences we share, the more sense of commonality and belonging we will feel.

One of my pastors, Kemp Holden, used to say, "You grow bigger by thinking smaller." He wasn't talking about limiting your dreams but by working toward connecting those in the large gathering on the weekend to a smaller setting. A church can grow infinitely large if it is comprised of small groups. If we gain significant relationships, we won't worry about the size of the crowd on the weekends. Our small group is where we begin to belong.

Accountability

One of the biggest growth barriers in our lives as Christians in America is a lack of accountability. We love to "go it alone." We don't want anyone to know we have issues. We're afraid that if we share who we really are people will tell someone else or leverage that information against us, but there is a power truth in scripture we can experience only when we have accountability in our lives. James reveals this truth:

> Confess your sins _to each other_ and pray for each other so that you may be healed. (James 5:16 NIV)

James reveals a powerful secret in this verse. We confess to God for forgiveness but to each other for healing.

If your first reaction is a refusal to have confession and accountability, I get it. This is scary. It is difficult to tell another human being the things that we've done wrong. After all, we don't know how they are going to react and respond. We wonder if they will reject us. We worry they might expose us to someone else. Even if the relationship is deep, it can be difficult to overcome feelings of shame in order to bring the secrets into the light.

My friend and fellow pastor, Alex Garro, helped me understand a spiritual concept hidden within this verse: until we make a confession of our sins to another human being, Satan holds power over us with our fear of being exposed. He taunts us with "What if they knew?" He blackmails us with a threat that he will expose us to others as a fraud and discredit us. For that reason, many of us do much less for God than He has called us to do because we're afraid of being discovered. We don't have the moral authority to move in confidence in the ministry God has given us, but when we confess and have the blessing of forgiveness from a fellow human being, our confidence and authority are restored.

We can grow to our full potential only with the aid of others.

The secondary benefit to confession is accountability. Once our area of struggle is exposed, our brothers and sisters can check up on us. The protection of accountability keeps us safe from our weaknesses and keeps us from stumbling in the same area over and over. We should develop a culture in our own hearts where we willingly "turn ourselves in" when we stumble into sin. When we place accountability in our lives, not only can we be forgiven by God, we can actually be healed.

This level of transparency isn't for the stage or for large groups. Not enough trust or relational credibility can be found there. This can happen only in the context of loving, deep, and trusting relationships. Small groups give us a place for these relationships to form.

For many of us this is the very thing that is holding us back from being a part of a small group. We know the time will come when we will have to decide if we really want to be real. We are not sure we want to "go there." Pastor Chris Hodges of Church of the Highlands says, "You'll always be as sick as your secrets." So let's not have any of those. Allow confession and accountability to set us free so we can fulfill everything God intended for us.

Growth

As soil is to vegetation, so are relationships to spiritual growth. We must be planted in life-giving relationships in order to grow in Christ. Many Christians think they can grow apart from community. This is simply not true.

We can grow to our full potential only with the aid of others. The California redwoods are an incredible demonstration of this truth. The roots of each tree do not grow very deep into the soil, but their roots intertwine with those of the surrounding trees. This network of roots provides a strength that allows the redwoods to grow more than 35 stories tall! One tree could never stand on its own, yet the entire forest supports itself.

In Ephesians 4, Paul gives us an illustration of how our lives are meant to be intertwined. He compares us to parts of a body. It's only when we join together in community as the body that we are able to grow to full maturity. Paul urges the church to become a close-knit community, a family. He says that when this happens

*Then **we will no longer be infants**, tossed back and forth by the waves, and **blown here and there by every wind of teaching** and by the cunning and craftiness of people in their deceitful scheming. Instead, speaking the truth in love, **<u>we will grow</u>** to become in every respect the mature body of him who is the head, that is, Christ. From him the whole body, **joined and held together by every supporting ligament**, **<u>grows</u>** and builds itself up in love, as each part does its work. (Ephesians 4:14-16 NIV)*

Community (being joined together) is required for us to grow! Many believers never take this step. They refuse to be a part of relationships that demand participation, care, belonging, and accountability. Some refuse because they've been wounded by past relationships, others because they refuse to submit to spiritual authority. Whatever the reason, living without community is to uproot ourselves from spiritual soil. We cannot grow if we are not planted.

Churches are filled with believers who have aged but have never matured in their relationship with God. They have grown but have not grown up. The result? As Paul described, they are infants tossed back and forth by waves of doctrine and the newest fads in church life. They spend their time chasing the latest new church experiences through revivals or the newest church in town. They never plant, and they never grow.

Growth happens best in groups.

Paul says growth will happen only when our lives are intertwined with others. It is simply impossible to grow alone. God never intended for us to do life alone. In fact more than 30 verses in the New Testament cannot be fulfilled outside community in the local church. The small group provides a context to facilitate community that allows us to be "planted" and grow.

John Wesley knew this years ago in the Methodist movement. He realized that preaching alone was not enough to help people grow into holiness and all that God intended for their lives. He developed "classes," which were none other than small groups. They provided a forum for sharing, accountability, and growth toward Godly character and values.

As Joel Comiskey writes, "John Wesley viewed preaching as the preamble of what would take place in the small groups. Discipleship took place in the lay-led class meetings through mutual ministry. The class meetings were Wesley's strategy for making disciples, rather than hearers of sermons."[13]

John Wesley saw the sermon as the preamble. It was the introduction, the catalyst for discipleship. Where did he believe discipleship happened most effectively? In a small group!

These "classes" were extremely effective in helping people grow to full maturity. As Dwight L. Moody said, "The class-meetings are the best institutions for training converts the world ever saw."[14]

Like the redwoods in California, we can grow substantially

when we place ourselves in the right environment, the soil of relationships. Once we intertwine our lives with others, the challenge of accountability, support, burden bearing, and a sense of belonging and family will produce more growth than Sunday alone. Growth happens best in groups.

Without a group you can avoid the difficulty of sharing others' burdens. You can slip in and slip out of the Sunday service anonymously. Sitting in a row, you can hide. You can avoid saying what the message spoke to you or even what the Holy Spirit is bringing conviction to in your life. You can check the box of churchgoing in your mind yet never come close to what it means to be a disciple of Christ. This is very dangerous, and it's what happens weekly in many churches as believers avoid the second environment that will cause them really to grow.

If we can get people into circles instead of rows only and if we get people face to face talking about the challenges of life and the tension of becoming all God intends, we will see incredible growth happen in our lives as disciples. We will see more of the gifts of the Spirit operate in our homes as we pray for one another. We will see more people share with one another as they did in the book of Acts. We will see people walk out of secret sins that have had them bound for years now that they have accountability and a family cheering them on to freedom.

Not only can this help the church grow deep in God, it can help us reach our friends for Christ—those who might find it outside their comfort zone to attend on a weekend. Their schedules and geographic locations could be additional complications that keep them from attending a service at the church, but a small group environment, hanging out with friends in your home, just might solve all those problems. Having a group at your house makes the church geographically and relationally easier for them to attend. It could take less than 3 minutes to get to a group at your house when your church building is 30 minutes across town.

What If?

What if the weekend service became an event of celebration rather than creation? What if we came together to rejoice over what God was already doing in and through the church? Imagine reports of people being saved in our homes instead of at the church! Imagine your small group tackling some community service project in your city without any prompting from the platform. Imagine what might happen when healings take place during your prayer times in your groups. Imagine a church where we count only the number of life groups instead of weekend attendance! What could happen if we caught the vision for getting in a circle, pursuing Jesus as a group, and spurring one another toward love and good deeds? What if we really believed this:

CIRCLES ARE BETTER THAN ROWS.

8

WE DON'T GET TO GET WHAT WE WANT

Nobody ever died of the wants.

- George Clarke

You wouldn't think that a little kid not getting a go-kart for Christmas would cause him to leave the ministry as an adult, but it did. That little wound was lurking under the surface waiting to reappear just at the wrong time.

I come from a humble beginning. My parents never made a lot money, so I didn't have much growing up other than an imagination. That wasn't a big deal. I found ways to entertain myself. From walking around in the woods and pastures around our house, playing with the dog, and reading books, I kept myself busy and entertained. Sometimes I would shoot cans with a BB gun; other times, I'd play with bottle rockets and firecrackers. Risky business.

I had a great imagination. I would make up stories and characters and then act out all the parts, capturing it all on a cassette tape recorder. My mom still has many of those tapes. Once she brought them out and played one or two for my kids. They thought they were the funniest recordings they had ever heard. They are entertained by them to this day.

Even though we didn't have a lot, I had all I needed–full belly, warm bed, roof over my head, and clothes on my back. I was a happy kid. My needs were met. Actually most of my wants were, too. My parents sacrificed a lot to make sure I could do the things I wanted. There was just this one thing. The thing I really wanted–*really* wanted–was a go-kart.

I don't think my parents ever knew I wanted the go-kart. I decided I would just tell God about it. You know, like Santa. I prayed for that go-kart for several Christmases. I prayed really hard. In my childish immaturity and understanding, I believed God not only heard me but that He wanted me to have a go-kart. It didn't seem like a want. It felt like a need. I imagined how awesome it would be to ride that go-kart up and down the long dirt road we lived on. Yet each Christmas came and went with no go-kart under the tree.

My childish mind didn't understand. Did God love me? Did He care for me? Was He listening? What did I do wrong? I could quote scriptures that I thought proved God wanted me to have it. So if God loved me and wanted to bless me, why didn't He give me that go-kart?

At some point I stopped thinking about that go-kart. As I grew up, I forgot all about even wanting it. It's funny now even writing about it. Without us knowing, however, such memories can be hidden deeply in our heart. These memories can frame and filter what you believe and how you trust God. As an adult I believed in God; I served God; I loved God; but somehow, somewhere, I didn't believe God wanted to bless me. After all, He didn't give me that go-kart. I suppose it really stuck with me. Buried deep in my heart, it became the symbol of a deep work God needed to do for me to be able to fulfill my purpose.

At age 14 I finally and fully gave my life to Jesus. I say it that way because, as a kid, I had been hot and cold over and over. We went to some very strict Pentecostal churches that preached that Hell was hot, and I was afraid to go there. In the summer when I was away from the influences of school, I would get red hot for Jesus. But about 4 weeks into school, I would try to out-sin my friends so they would think I was cool. I had no ability to stand strong in my relationship with God.

In the summer of 1987, I fully surrendered to Jesus and immediately felt that I was called into ministry. I wanted to be a pastor on staff at a church. I wanted people to get saved and experience the life and love of Jesus. I stood at the altar in my church with tears streaming down my face begging God to call me to into ministry. It was a burning passion. All I wanted was to serve God in ministry. I cashed in my whole future. Whatever the cost, whatever it took, I promised I would serve God, and I did.

To pursue the call to ministry, I changed everything! I arranged my classes, my extracurricular activities, and my work schedule to accommodate this high priority in my life. I would allow nothing to get in the way of my calling. As I was faithful, I continued to receive favor with God and man. I have never sought ministry positions; they have always found me. God was faithful.

Aimee and I wanted four kids. People told us that children

were expensive, but I guess we just ignored them. We both had always wanted a large family. Having a large family and a small paycheck means you have to do some extra things in order to feed all those mouths you brought into the world. Both of us did, willfully and pleasantly (most of the time).

As was the norm for ministry, we didn't have large salaries. If I was paid well at a church, it was usually because I was assigned multiple positions on staff. To make ends meet, one or both of us typically worked an extra job outside the church. We were usually stretched thin, wondering if there would be month left at the end of the money.

As time went on and we became more weary, I grew frustrated. I knew something needed to change, so when I was introduced to an opportunity to sell insurance and investments as a part-time gig on the side, it got my attention. I was always looking for a way to make a buck, but this was the promise of making thousands of those bucks each month as a part-time person. I could still keep my day job as a pastor and sell insurance and investments on the side.

That's exactly what we did. I was pastor by day, salesman by night. I began making quite a bit of extra cash. Everything was going really well. Then I realized I could make a lot *more* money if I *didn't* keep my day job. I started thinking, "What if I did this full-time?" I could make loads of money; then I could give a lot to the church and help fund ministry. I was convinced it was a great plan. I began to think financial independence was just around the corner. Did you catch that word? "Independence?" Yeah, that one was the one that got me.

See, even though my plan seemed good, pure, and even noble, there was something beneath it I didn't recognize. Somewhere buried in my subconscious was a desire that I didn't even know I had. It was expressed in the image of a go-kart I was never given. If God could not be trusted to give a little boy a simple inexpensive go-kart, how could He be trusted to care for a man and his family of six? What I failed to realize was that I simply did not trust God. What I wanted was not riches. What I wanted was freedom from dependence on God.

The business I sold insurance and investments for produced shirts that bore the slogan "I will thrive in 2005." I believed it. That slogan became a mantra for me. "I will thrive in 2005." *I* will thrive. I bought the T-shirt and the philosophy. I was going to be rich. I was going to be independent–not just financially independent, but totally independent. Somehow I was going to make sure I didn't need God to provide for me any more. I would take care of it on my own.

This idea began to work its way out into real life. After I began working for that company part-time, Aimee and I started feeling that God might be calling us to leave church staff and pursue this new career in the marketplace. We prayed and asked God to give us a sign if we were to make this huge step of faith. Confirmation after confirmation began to point us in that direction. As we were seeking direction, we went to a church-growth conference in Georgia. This conference normally focuses on the church and how we can do a better job at leading it. Somehow the focus that year was on leading in the marketplace. We believed this was yet another confirmation that God wanted us to leave staff and pursue this venture. He was in it. He was with us. He was going to bless us. We were going to be wealthy.

Little did we know that God was leading us into this venture for a purpose far different from what I imagined. I had no idea what He was really up to. I thought I was going to get rich, but what I got was far different. While I had visions and dreams of financial independence, God was leading me toward a moment that would mark my life forever.

We left our church staff and began pursuing selling insurance and investments. My dream to make money turned quickly to a nightmare. I worked and worked to make sales. Somehow it seemed that each significant sale I made would cancel, change, or fall through on some decision, technicality, or hiccup. It was exasperating! I watched sale after sale evaporate. Money was getting tighter and tighter. I thought we might go under.

During this time, God supernaturally provided for us. Aimee was able to get a job doing medical transcription, a field for which she had zero training or experience. Typically you cannot get a job in this field without college training, but she got it anyway. She excelled tremendously. Her medical transcription job kept us afloat as I went through the income drought. We were still dependent on God. He was providing, just not the way I wanted.

While she was working this job, I would often wake up at 2 or 3 a.m. to find Aimee at the keyboard typing. This was the time of day that transcription work was available for her. As she sat trying to understand the foreign doctors and transcribe what they were saying, I felt shame, guilt, anger, and jealousy. I felt as if I had led us into a desert to die. I was sad and depressed. I was humiliated. I was supposed to be the provider. Now my wife was providing while I lay in the bed sleeping. I felt like the biggest loser in the world.

I had thought, "This is it!" I was going to thrive. I would make millions, tithe to the church, and relieve the strain on their ministry. Everyone would win in this scenario. My kids would get a go-kart or whatever "need" they had, but it didn't happen. The more things trekked along, the more I felt like that little boy on Christmas morning looking outside for the go-kart. Only this time I was a man looking for daily bread. I wondered how we were going to make it through. I wondered if God cared. I wondered if He knew.

I felt *entitled* to God's blessing.

It Came From Within

During this time I was given a book written by Andy Stanley entitled *It Came From Within*, which deals with four enemies of the heart: Guilt, Anger, Greed, and Jealousy.

As I read the book, I was struggling. I felt that God had led us into this wilderness. We were here because of Him. He had led us this direction. He told us this was the way to go. Yet once we obeyed and stepped out in faith, it was like He had stopped speaking. I could no longer hear His voice. I didn't even know if He was there. I had no answers to my questions. Why were we here? Why did these deals keep falling through? When would things turn around?

I continued reading Andy's book. When I got to the part that deals with jealousy, God started speaking. He spoke clearly and in a way that made everything crystal clear. He revealed why He had led us to leave the church staff to pursue this venture into the marketplace.

It had nothing to do with getting rich or famous or with becoming financially independent. It had nothing to do with me being able to provide money for church ministries. It was something completely different. I probably could have understood it sooner if I had been looking, but I guess I really never was.

As I continued reading this specific chapter, I was ambushed by the Holy Spirit through Andy's writings. An excerpt reads as follows:

> From the beginning of time, jealousy has played a featured role in the story of human relationships. Cain was jealous of Abel. Esau was jealous of Jacob. Joseph's brothers were jealous of their younger brother's relationship with Dad. Commodus was jealous of Maximus and his relationship with Commodus's father, the emperor of Rome. Woody felt replaced by Buzz. When we think of jealousy, we think of the things others have that we lack—looks, talent, health, height, money, connections, and so on. And so we think we have a problem with the person who possesses what we lack. But as we've said, God could have fixed all of that. Whatever he's given to your neighbor, he could have chosen to give you as well. But what we fail to see is that our problem isn't REALLY with the people whose stuff you envy; it's with

God. Because He could have done the same thing for you that He did for them, but He did not.[15]

The Reckoning

As I was reading this part of the chapter, I was stretched out on my stomach on our bed. I remember this moment so clearly. In a flash of truth, God confronted the ugly reality lodged deep in my heart: **I felt *entitled* to God's blessing**. I didn't even realize it. I knew in the back of my mind that I had wanted a go-kart as a kid, but I didn't realize that not getting one had shaped my view of God.

Please understand that many factors in my relationship with God and my upbringing skewed and distorted my view, but the image of this one stands out. It's a picture that helps me understand clearly what was going on in my heart. Hopefully it paints a picture for you, too. Maybe you, too, had an experience that tarnished your view of God as a child. Imagine a little boy, still longing for that go-kart, making a vow to Himself that He will never have to depend on a God that doesn't answer his prayers.

I felt that God owed me a go-kart. I had felt slighted all these years. The real issue was that I felt *entitled* to what I asked for. I felt that I worked hard for God. I gave up things. I had chosen to follow Him. Looking around at other people, I could justify (to myself) how much more I deserved His blessing than they did. And the question floated under the surface, "WHY WON'T YOU BLESS ME LIKE YOU BLESS THEM?!"

God doesn't owe me. God owns me.

The Woodshed

As I lay there with all this realization unfolding in a moment, my Heavenly Father took me to the spiritual woodshed. I wept and wept as he lovingly and forcefully disciplined me. He spoke truth in love. He began to confront and cast out the lie in my heart that had kept me from real relationship with Him. I have never felt stronger discipline in my life. It was painful. Yet at the same time, I have never felt more comfort. As I was scolded and disciplined, the true nature of my heart was exposed. The ugliness of what had been buried in my heart was revealed. I was embarrassed, I was ashamed, yet I never have felt more secure than in that moment. As God was disciplining me, He was holding me close.

I realized that all along I had felt that God owed me. I was still that little boy on Christmas morning begging God for the go-kart. Since he didn't get one for me, I decided I would simply do my best to take Him out of the equation. Sure, I would trust Him with my salvation, but there was *no way* I would trust Him with the things that were in my control. I would make enough money to cut Him out of the deal. I would provide my family with the nicest things, the best insurance, the best medical care, college tuition, cars–all the things money could buy. I didn't want to depend on God.

The Realization

As God exposed this lie, He gave a troubling and comforting truth at the same time. He began to tell me, "**Jon, I don't owe you anything**." That's the lie of jealousy. We think God owes us something. He should fix it. He needs to give us a better life. He needs to heal us. We deserve it.

God kept speaking to me, "I don't owe you an explanation. I don't have to promise you that your kids will outlive you. I don't have to promise you that you will have a retirement fund or a retirement at all. I don't have to promise you that you won't be disabled. I don't have to promise you that your wife will grow old with you. I don't owe you an explanation if you don't have everything you need, everything you want, or even if your basic human needs are not being met. I gave you Jesus. I bought you through His death on the cross. That is more than enough." I came face to face with this truth: God doesn't **owe** me. God **owns** me.

The lie was stripped away. The wound laid open, surgery done, and cancer extracted from my very soul. I came to the realization in that moment that God really *did* love me and He had a plan that was larger than my life here on Earth. I discovered that He loved me no matter what happened and that I could trust Him no matter where His path took me. I have a loving Father who is free to use my life just as He wills.

He's not willing to be Savior only. He must also be Lord.

This is the realization that you and I must come to if we are to be used in the Kingdom for God's purpose in the Earth: God owns us.

Don't you realize that your body is the temple of the Holy Spirit, who lives in you and was given to you by God? ***You do not belong to yourself, for God bought*** *you with a high price. So you must honor God with your body. (1 Corinthians 6:19-20 NLT)*

Yes, He loves us; yes, He cares for us; and yes, He is free to use our lives as He chooses. The shed blood of Jesus Christ on the cross bought us from the slavery of our sin, but it does not simply make Him our Savior. It also makes Him our Lord. If we are honest, most of us don't like that "lord" part. We are fine with Jesus being our savior. We are thankful that He's rescued us from sin and Hell; however, it is not an either-or proposition but a both-and. He's not willing to be Savior only; He must also be Lord.

I Give Myself Away

We no longer belong to ourselves. God needs us to choose to give our lives away. As you choose to become a Second Mile Leader in the church, people will disappoint you. They will criticize you, hurt you, betray you, and perhaps even stab you in the back, but if we start this whole thing with the realization that our lives are not our own, we won't have as much to defend in the first place. Our lives don't belong to us anyway, do they?

**Surrender to God means giving up
our rights to determine outcomes.**

In the fourth chapter of James, he asks us a question that seems so open ended it couldn't possibly have just one answer: "What causes fights and quarrels among you?"

What is causing the quarrels and fights among you? Don't they come from the evil desires at war within you? You want what you don't have, so you scheme and kill to get it. You are jealous of what others have, but you can't get it, so you fight and wage war to take it away from them. Yet you don't have what you want because you don't ask God for it. And even when you ask, you don't get it because your motives are all wrong—you want only what will give you pleasure. (James 4:1-3 NLT)

James is essentially saying this: "We don't get to get what we want."

My motives for wanting the go-kart seemed innocent to me, and they probably were. I don't think I was really going to do any damage to relationships or subvert God's purpose in my life. I don't know why I never got the go-kart. Perhaps God knew I would wreck it and kill myself before I could accomplish his purpose in my life. What I *do* know is this: God used that memory to probe the depths of my heart to reveal every part that was not surrendered to Him. Upon finding those parts, He promptly did heart surgery to align me with His will and His purpose. I realized I had a false idea of God in my heart that was stopping me from fulfilling His purpose.

So what is that for you? What is standing in the way of you becoming a Second Mile Leader, someone that is fully surrendered to God's will and purpose for your life? Is it your career? Is it independence? Is it a relationship? Perhaps it is an award or accolade you've had your heart set on for years. Whatever it is, it's time to let it go. It's time to realize that surrender to God means giving up our rights to determine outcomes. God demands full obedience. Paul says it like this in Romans 12:

> *Therefore I urge you, brethren, by the mercies of God,* to **present your bodies a living and holy sacrifice,** *acceptable to God,* **which is your spiritual service of worship**. *(Romans 12:1 NAS)*

When we think "worship," we think about singing songs, and while we do worship with song, those songs don't really mean anything if our lives don't back them up. Paul says the real way we worship is to give our bodies to God as a tool in His hands, ready to be used for whatever He desires. That's *real* worship.

It's worship when you serve someone and they "use you." You know, that person who calls only when he needs something, that person who borrowed money and didn't return it, that one that asked your advice and didn't follow it, the one who used something you created and didn't give you credit. Whatever it was they did, you felt "used."

It's interesting how we ask God to use us and then get upset when people do. Remember–that's the only way God *can* use us. He uses us to serve people. We have to remember that there isn't anything that God needs. He isn't hungry. He isn't thirsty. He said though that when we give a cup of cold water to a little one in His name, it's as though we are doing it to Him.

When we moved to take a position at CT Church in Houston, we sang a song in service that I had never heard before. It became one of my favorite songs because it brought me back to that moment when I lay across the bed and gave everything back to God. This song was God confirming that this was the next step in His journey for our lives as a family. These are the lyrics:

> I give myself away / I give myself away so you can use me
> I give myself away / I give myself away so you can use me
> My life is not my own / to you I belong
> I give myself / I give myself away [16]

I stood in the Sunday night service, surrounded by the presence of God as he said, "Remember. Remember, I don't owe you. I own you. Give yourself away to these people."

I wonder if that's the cry of your heart. "God, use me." If you have read this far in this book, I'm sure it is. Let's ask Him now to use us however, wherever, whenever He wants.

In order for us to be useful as we progress into what God has for us and is calling us into, we must remember this: We are not our own; we were bought with a price. Our worship is our bodies being given in service to God. We don't get to live our lives for ourselves anymore. They must be surrendered to His will.

WE DON'T GET TO GET WHAT WE WANT.

9

THE FOUR C'S

Try not to become a person of success,
but rather try to become a person of value.
- Albert Einstein

There are a few things I can do well. Plumbing is not one of them. I hate it with a passion. I believe that when we get to Heaven we will find out the devil himself invented it. This belief is reinforced every single time I do a plumbing repair project at my house. No matter how hard I try or what I buy at the store I always have problems. When I try to solder copper pipes, they leak. When I fix a drain, it leaks. When I buy fittings for pipe connections at the hardware store, I drive home only to find it's the wrong one. I end up going back and forth to the hardware store seemingly a dozen times. I try to get the right part so that my pipes will fit together and by some magic not leak! One 25¢ part costs me about $30 in fuel, 4 hours of frustration, and one prayer of repentance for the things I thought and said.

I know (by *experience*) that if things don't fit together well the water that is supposed to go into the drain ends up on the floor.

Making everything fit together properly is extremely important.

Proper fittings aren't important just in plumbing; they are important for church leaders. As we become placed as Second Mile Leaders, we must find our fit. There's a lot at stake. Ephesians tells us why:

> *Rather, speaking the truth in love, we are to grow up in every way into him who is the head, into Christ, from whom the whole body, **joined and held together by every joint** with which it is equipped, **when each part is working properly, makes the body grow so that it builds itself up in love**. (Ephesians 4:15-16 ESV)*

Paul says that the whole body is held together by every joint. That means every single relational connection is important. The value of what we offer the world flows only when the whole body is held together. It takes only a single failure of relationship to cause damage to the cause of Christ.

When we launched a second campus for the Journey Church in Clarksville, Arkansas, we did extensive renovations. We installed a refrigerator that needed a water supply, so we tapped the waterline underneath the sink. The fitting wasn't installed properly, and it failed. One morning just before our grand opening, our new campus pastors came to the building to find about 2 inches of water throughout the lobby and into the auditorium. The fitting, which had cost less than $2, ruined the flooring, baseboards, and sheetrock. The campus then needed to undergo a hurried, expensive renovation before we opened the campus. That was not a happy day, and it was all caused by something that didn't fit together the way it was designed.

In this scripture Paul says that we are designed perfectly so we will fit together. We are not placed together because we are the same, but because we are *different*. Each of us has a fit and a function in the body. In another passage Paul describes how ridiculous our bodies would look if they were made up of only one part:

> *If the whole body were an eye, where would the sense of hearing be? If the whole body were an ear, where would the sense of smell be? (1 Corinthians 12:17 NIV)*

Our bodies work because they are made up of *different* parts. The same goes for the people in our churches. We are different by design. Paul says it's only when each part is working properly that the body builds itself up in love.

Leaders rise above the tension that comes from differences.

As a Second Mile Leader, you have to embrace the tension this difference brings. The differences God has around you are purposeful and healthy. God needs you to connect with people who don't act like you or think like you. Some people rub us the wrong way. They get on our nerves. They bug us with their political views and opinions. Good heavens, they even chew ice! Oh, the humanity!

Sometimes we feel like we are forcing the relationship. While it's true of magnets that opposites attract, it's not always true of relationships. Sometimes I don't like you because I'm not like you. But leaders rise above the tension that comes from differences. They know something big is at stake. The world needs the body of Christ to function the way it was intended.

We live in Houston, Texas, next to chemical plants that refine petroleum or manufacture the by-products of petroleum. To accomplish these processes, the plants use chemicals that are major health hazards. If some of these chemicals leak, thousands of people could die. If other chemicals leak, explosions could destroy homes and kill people. The integrity of the pipes and fittings that contain these chemicals is critically important. Lives are at stake.

When church people are unable to fit together properly as Paul describes, however, something much more valuable is lost–eternal lives! We are the conduit for God's power and presence. He moves through us when we are connected to one another. If we break apart, *people* are lost. For eternity.

Jesus calls us to a higher standard—one in which we lay down our rights and pick up our obligations.

As a Second Mile Leader, our view of the relationships around us must change. Average church attenders may get their feelings hurt. They may refuse to forgive. They may choose to leave when things get tough. But we cannot. As leaders we must realize that holding tight to those connections God has given us is critical. While others may want to run from relational fractures, we run toward them.

While people may be letting off steam and hurling insults, we keep our cool. We are working to restore, not inflame. This is a foreign concept to us. We are so used to defending ourselves, our reputations. We are so used to choosing what we do with our lives. We get to control what we do and when we do it, but Jesus calls us to a higher standard—one in which we lay down our rights and pick up our obligations—our cross.

This is so clear when Jesus restores Peter. After Jesus restores Peter, He gives him this foreboding honor:

> *"Very truly I tell you, when you were younger you dressed yourself and went where you wanted; but when you are old you will stretch out your hands, and someone else will dress you and lead you where you do not want to go." Jesus said this to indicate the kind of death by which Peter would glorify God. Then he said to him, "Follow me!" (John 21:18-19 NIV)*

Jesus foretold how Peter's death would glorify God. Peter would be willing to go all the way in following Jesus. He would lay down every right he had in order to remain faithful to the pledge he made to Jesus: "Yes, Lord, I love you."

Jesus told Peter that the young rash, selfish Peter made all the decisions for his life but that the old wise, selfless Peter would be taken where he didn't want to go. And Peter would willingly go where he wouldn't want to go.

The issue with many of us who follow Christ is that we never come face to face with the full surrender of our wills to Christ. We want to do things our way. We want to defend ourselves, but we really need to be defending the cause of Christ in the world.

As Second Mile Leaders, we are going to deal with a little friction in our lives–a little tension at the connections. We're not always going to be able to get to be right. In fact, the higher you go in leadership the fewer rights you have. As a Second Mile Leader, we need to come face to face with this reality early on: I must surrender my rights and shoulder my responsibilities. I have to be more about "us" being right than "me" being right. The relationship is more important.

You may be balking at these ideas right now. I get it. I've been doing this a long time and still don't like it. When you have to swallow your pride and apologize because of something you've done wrong, it's not fun, but it's even more humbling when you have to take it on the chin when you know you are right. You know it's more important to salvage the relationship than your pride. As leaders we can't afford to be offendable or offensive; we have to help others connect.

Making Connections

To lead people we must be able to connect relationally. This is easy when people are agreeable, cheerful, and pleasant. It gets difficult when we don't share the same interests and ideas. Many of us would like to choose those we connect with and those we don't. As leaders we no longer get that luxury. At our church we say it like this:

This is a place where anyone from anywhere who's done anything can find hope, help, and healing in Jesus.

Over the years I've watched plenty of people in the church define who is welcome in their circles and who is not. I get it. Sometimes I would like to be able to do that as well, but I can't. I have a higher responsibility–to shepherd those God puts in my path. As a Second Mile Leader, so do you.

So how can we make sure we can fit together in relationships with others? When you assemble two pieces of plumbing, components are typically added to the raw material to cause them to adhere to one another. Without these substances, they would fit, but they wouldn't be connected. Relationships have intangible substances that help them connect and stick as well. While there are many, I would like to explore four of them.

The Four C's

There are four C's that really define what makes us great at relationships. They cause us to become great team members and leaders. When I hire people, I do my best to to make sure they have all four of these. If I bring new leaders into positions in our organization, I want to make sure they have them.

To connect well with others, you need these four elements in the relationship. A deficiency or a lack of one of these will surface sooner or later. Without them structural failures will occur in your leadership and those you are connected to. Disconnections will cause relationships to fail. Your teams and circles of influence will "leak" people. Your influence will shrink.

Character

Character is your internal quality. A person of character is first and foremost trustworthy. We all have people in our lives that we struggle to trust. There is either "just something about them" or something they have done that makes us feel we simply cannot trust them.

Perhaps as you read this, a certain person comes your mind. What is it that makes you not trust them? Is it an attitude or a previous action? Are they totally untrustworthy, or is it that they cannot be trusted in one particular area? It's interesting, because we generally can point to an incident with people in which a particular breach of trust happened. From that point on the person is marked. We may forgive them, but we refuse to trust them.

Trust

In order for you to lead people, they need to trust you. They need to know that you will be there for them. If you currently serve on a team, trustworthiness might look like showing up on time each time you are scheduled. If you forget or bail on responsibilities, your team will stop trusting you.

In a relationship trustworthiness might mean picking up the phone consistently when someone calls. They know they can count on you when things are not going well for them. People can trust you to keep their weaknesses and shame covered. They believe you are the type of person who won't let a secret slip or, worse yet, delightfully share the latest gossip about their lives.

Reliability

A person of character is reliable. We've all seen the illustration of someone who goes out on a limb only to have it break. The limb might have looked strong, but under the pressure and weight it broke.

Many people seem reliable, but they simply have no follow-through. They are similar to the parable Jesus told about the seed that falls on the rocky soil. They spring up quickly. They are excited about the new project or initiative but are nowhere to be found just a few days in. They fail to follow through on commitments when it gets hard. They are not reliable.

People who have no follow-through are not leadership material. People will not follow someone who doesn't follow through. Leaders with no "stick-to-it-ive-ness" have no one who will follow them. Their team knows they will leave if things get tough. Our character comes into question when people discover they cannot rely on us.

Your gifting will take you only as far as your character can sustain you.

Integrity

A person of character has integrity. Public me and private me need to be the same. Stage me and backstage me need to be the same. We need to be who we portray ourselves to be. It should be genuine, not fake.

In Greek theaters the actors on stage were called "hypocrites." They pretended to be someone they were not. We have to ask ourselves constantly if the self we allow people to see is who we really are.

This doesn't mean we don't fail. As long as we are on this side of Heaven, we will have times when we stumble and fall short of what we proclaim to be and believe. An authentic person confesses it, repents, and moves forward in transparency. Hypocrites ignore or cover failures, pretending they didn't happen. That's called being fake. People hate a fake!

Quality

People of character have quality. They have a deep reliance on God. They have a devotion to God that guides their lives and decisionmaking. A person that has quality will make the decisions that place God first, others second, and self last. A person without quality is simply in it for himself.

Effective leaders are people of character. Many gifted people have risen quickly to leadership in church and business, but gifting must be backed by character or we will fall. Your gifting will take you only as far as your character can sustain you.

Competence

Competence is our ability to do something based on our knowledge or skill.

A funny movie titled *Joe Versus the Volcano* is about a man named Joe whose entire existence is miserable. He has no purpose, no joy, and no hope. In the opening scene Joe walks into his office at the company he hates. As he enters we can hear the misery of meaningless being verbalized by his boss in the background. The boss is on a phone call continuously repeating, "I know he can *get* the job, but can he *do* the job?" The scene is hilarious, but the question the boss is asking is one every boss or leader is asking about his next selection, promotion, or hire: "I know he can get the job, but can he *do* the job?"

**It is much easier to refine your gifting
than to try to develop one you don't have.**

This question is at the core of the second C. It's one your leader or pastor is asking himself before giving you a position, title, or keys. He can give you the job, but can you do the job?

This question has nothing to do with our character. It is not about reliability or integrity. This is all about skill and aptitude. To lead well, we have to have the skill or ability to learn to do what we are asked by our leaders. We need not only to be able to learn but also to be able to receive coaching. Great team members and leaders are willing to ask for input. They love constructive criticism and feedback. They want to get better.

Many times our pride gets in the way of our next step of growth because we are afraid of looking weak or incompetent. Yet our willingness to acknowledge and address our deficits actually bolster the confidence of those around us.

We know that a know-it-all is not the kind of person we want on our team. John Maxwell says, "Until you know what you don't know, you can't grow." We need to be people who are willing to be questioned and who ask questions to find better ways to do things.

Competent people have a drive to get better at what they are doing. They have a spirit of excellence that says, "Today was good; tomorrow can be better." Are you pushing yourself to learn more and be better? I am constantly listening to other sermons and messages, trying to find better ways to communicate. I go to conferences and leadership trainings to learn from others who do it better. Having a spirit of excellence causes you to want to grow and increases the second C, Competence. Find ways to get better at what you do. Ask for constructive criticism and feedback. Find a mentor who is two steps beyond you. Without this in your life, you'll be stuck where you are.

Know your core competency. As Paul says, everyone has a gift, a role, and a part in the body. Do what you are designed to do, not what you desire to do. It is much easier to refine your gifting than to try to develop one you don't have. Find whatever God has created you to be and constantly improve in that area.

Culture

Culture is the DNA, vision, values, and philosophy of your particular organization. Having the same culture means you are headed in the same direction. If we add another vision to the mix of what our pastor or boss wants, it's di-vision–two visions. To be trusted by your leadership you need to have the same culture. While it is beneficial to have a different perspective, it's unhealthy to have a different vision. It is imperative for you to be able to get on the same page as your leader. If you cannot support the culture of the organization, you should not become a leader.

When I started implementing the Second Mile Leadership at my campus, it was culture shock. Some did not see what I saw. Others did not agree with the culture I was seeking to establish. A few families left. One family in particular was very honoring in the way they left the church. They communicated that they simply did not have the same philosophy. They were not upset, but they wanted to find a place where they felt more aligned. I thanked them for handling the situation honorably.

Since I began leading this campus, I have worked to establish new culture and set of values. My goal is to lead every single person in the church to be a minister, actively seeking to reconcile men to God in their daily lives. My desire is to see a small group in every neighborhood in our cities. I'm determined to put a campus in every neighborhood. I'm determined to celebrate on the weekend what is happening in the church on the weekdays. It has been hard work to establish this culture. I do not want someone on my team who has different values or who is pulling the church into a different philosophy.

Do you have the DNA of the organization or church that you're part of? Your church can't afford division in leadership. There can be only one vision, or people will be hurt as they are pulled in two separate directions. Division in leadership is harmful. You and I must serve under the authority God has placed in our lives.

I myself am a man under authority, with soldiers under me. I tell this one, 'Go,' and he goes; and that one, 'Come,' and he comes. I say to my servant, 'Do this,' and

he does it."
(Matthew 8:9 NIV)

The Roman soldier knew the source of his authority. His ability to command came from his alignment with a higher authority. We have authority when we are under a higher authority. We are authorized to lead as we are in agreement with the commands that come from higher up; therefore, if you cannot agree with the direction of your higher authorities, you should not lead.

Most people are smart enough to realize when we are not aligned with the authorities above us. If they sense that we are going a different direction than the rest of the leadership, they will disconnect from our leadership. They will not stick around with a person who has a different culture. When it comes to culture, you can participate without sharing the same culture, but you cannot lead without adhering to it.

Chemistry

If you're like me, you've probably had people in your life whom you liked just fine, but for some reason you just didn't connect. Maybe you felt like you just didn't "click" or "gel." For some reason, you struggled to take the conversation much beyond small talk.

As a Second Mile Leader, you are required to be the type of person that others desire to hang around. After all, the whole goal of leadership is influence, and our leadership is aimed at taking people into a deeper commitment to Jesus. We can't do that if they don't want to hang around us.

Chemistry is that intangible thing that just makes you enjoy being with someone. Perhaps they set you at ease. Maybe they inspire you to be a better person. Maybe they make you laugh. Or maybe they make you believe in yourself when no one else ever has. Whatever it is about this person, your connection with them is this intangible thing called "chemistry."

Just as there are things that can draw us toward people, there are a few negative traits that will always push people away from us. It will ruin the chemistry. As you look at these next traits, see if any of the personalities or descriptions fit you.

Negative Neil

Neil's outlook is simple. When others see a silver lining, he's quick to point out that it's just hiding a very dark cloud. This guy finds a problem with every possibility. He's the Eeyore to Winnie the Pooh. Oh, bother! He brings everyone down. People won't bother with a relationship with this guy. They will run for the hills to stay away from Negative Neil.

Reclusive Renee

This lady loves her personal space, and *all* her space is personal. She wonders why in the world you would call when a simple text message will do. It's hard to get together with Renee because she doesn't like to be together. If you tell her she's not meant to do life alone, she points you to where God said it's not good for *man* to be alone. He said man, not woman, she says, and she's perfectly fine, thank you.

The problem with Renee is access. She's probably a terrific person with lots of wisdom, love, and care to give. But whether she's just a selfish person or is filled with social anxiety, you'll never be able to access her. She going to be at home. Alone.

Motormouth Michelle

Michelle loves to use the words. All of them. She says so many words so quickly that you aren't even able to let her know you've fallen asleep. You can't get a word in with Michelle, edgewise or otherwise. Her incessant talking communicates a subtle truth, whether she means it or not. It's the truth that "you are not important."

Unless you're a person who doesn't want to talk at all, this is annoying. People want to share their story, contribute to the conversation, and be valued. Talking over someone constantly communicates that you don't care what they have to say or value what they bring to the relationship. Michelle's friends have to find someone else who will let them share what is happening in their lives.

God gave us two two ears and one mouth. This is an anatomical clue to remind us we should listen twice as much as we speak. When we listen twice as much, people *like* us twice as much.

Boastful Bob

Bob loves to talk as much as Michelle, but Bob wants to talk about only one subject. Bob. Bob brags constantly about all Bob's accomplishments. While Bob is probably just compensating for Bob feeling insecure, the result is that Bob minimizes others and makes them feel small in the process. Bob is what the comedian Brian Regan describes as a "me monster."

There's an old adage about relationships: Share a success; build a wall. Share a failure; build a bridge. We would be wise to take this to heart. People connect with us more when share our struggles than when we boast of our successes. It gives them a "me too" moment. They realize they are not alone in their struggle. They have a fellow human being who understands them and can help overcome their problems.

When you talk to others, make sure you also listen. Don't just talk about you; talk about them. Try building them up, not yourself. Develop a genuine interest in others. Become a resource for their success.

Strange Stanley

You know that weird uncle that you don't want to see at Thanksgiving but who's always there? That's Stanley. He's the guy people "forget" to inform when they are taking the family photo. People hang out with Stanley only because they have to.

Why? Stanley is *weird*, and he's a little creepy. When you're around him, you feel uneasy. You never know what he's going to talk about; you just know it will be either odd, uncomfortable, or polarizing. Stanley might not be just *weird*; he might be *super-spiritual* weird. Everything is an angel or a demon. Every conversation goes somewhere strange.

When people see Stanley at the grocery store, they pretend they forgot something on another aisle. At another store. People avoid Stanley at all costs. Don't be a Stanley.

Being weird because "that's just who I am" isn't very considerate of the call and purpose God has on our lives. We have to find a way to temper our personalities and "fit in," not because we're looking for approval but for connection.

Paul said, "I have become all things to all people so that by all possible means I might save some" (1 Corinthians 9:22 NIV). We have to meet people where they are, not where we are. It's about them, not me.

A final note about chemistry. Without it, you can't bond! We all had those labs in high school that we don't remember anymore. What we do know, however, is that chemical reactions happen when the right ingredients are in the right proportion in the right environment, and we want our chemistry to foster connections. Not because we want people to connect with us but to God.

Maybe you wonder if you have one of the negative personality traits above. Be humble and ask people. Listen to their perspective on the way you interact with others. Don't get your feelings hurt; thank them for their feedback. A little bit of feedback could make you a life-giving person.

The Missing C's

It's important that we have all the C's. If we have any C's missing, we will end up missing a portion or all of our calling. Having all four is important because one without the other can prove to be a major lid on a leader's life.

- Culture + Chemistry + Competence without Character = deadly
- Character + Culture + Chemistry without Competence = faulty
- Chemistry + Competence + Character without Culture = division
- Character + Competence + Culture without Chemistry = lonely

Let's strive to be leaders that have Character, Competence, Culture, and Chemistry. If we have these traits, we will be able to connect with others, make investments in their lives, and see them grow closer to Christ.

10

WATCH YOUR ATTITUDE

Boy, you better watch your attitude!

- Ida Nell Ashcraft

This may come as a surprise, but many times as a child I would get very unhappy about what Mom or Dad told me to do. When I expressed my displeasure, frequently I would be told, "Boy, you better watch your attitude!" The tone in *Mom's* voice told me that the tone in *my* voice was unacceptable. Further it let me know that if it didn't change soon, I might have to do something extremely humiliating–cut my own switch.

It's bad enough to get a spanking. It's a whole new level of humiliation when you have to cut your own spanking tool and carry it to your mom. I didn't like doing that, so the threat was usually enough to fix my attitude. Maybe that's what is wrong with our culture right now–kids no longer have to cut their own switches when they get too big for their britches.

A few years ago I was on the receiving end of someone who had apparently never had to have an attitude adjustment. It wasn't a great experience.

I was spending the day hanging out with one of my children. On the way to our destination, I realized I needed to put fuel in my car. I pulled into the gas station and filled it. Back then you could actually pump your gas, then pay, and that's exactly what I did. I filled the tank and went inside to pay for the fuel. When I reached for my wallet, I realized I didn't have it.

I immediately told the clerk behind the counter I had forgotten my wallet but had no intention of leaving until I had someone deliver it so I could pay. I made a phone call to my wife asking her to bring me my wallet and waited for her to arrive.

In the midst of all the conversations and trying to make things right, I completely forgot to move my car from the pumps. I just sat down at a table with my kid and waited.

Unbeknownst to be, my failure to move my car completely ruined another guy's day. He came in several minutes later to pay for his fuel and make his purchases. He angrily asked whose car was outside at the pumps, stating that he had hit the car with his trailer trying to get past it to get fuel.

I told him it was my car he had struck with his vehicle and began the conversation to discuss insurance coverage. Instead of working out the damages, he went on and on about how all this was my fault and how I should have moved my car. I was trying to be kind and resolve the situation, but he wasn't having it. I was starting to get angry. His attitude was ticking me off.

Finally I said, "Sir, I think you're just upset because you've made a mistake, but there's no reason to act like this." He promptly responded, "I didn't hit your car; I was just trying to find out what jerk left their car parked there."

Now I was completely fuming. Granted, I had done a thoughtless thing. In trying to avoid getting a ticket for driving off from the pumps and communicate with the clerk, I had completely forgotten about leaving my car at the pump. I didn't even think about pulling the car out of the way of the vehicles behind me.

Sure, I should have moved, but this jerk's attitude was completely uncalled for. Apparently he was having a terrible day and wanted to make sure everyone else around him had one, too. His sour attitude rubbed off on me. By the time this ridiculous interaction was over, I was hot and ready for a fight!

Have you ever met someone like this guy? Maybe it was someone whose hobby is to rub people the wrong way. Maybe it was someone with a chip on his shoulder who was always looking to pick a fight. Have you met someone who perpetually woke up on the wrong side of the bed or met someone you instantly knew you'd never like? Have you ever had someone create a first impression of himself that you didn't think you could ever get over? If so, you know what it's like to come face to face with a bad attitude.

The Secret Ingredient

Attitudes, perhaps more than anything else in life, determine how far we can go with people, how much we can endure, and ultimately whether we succeed or fail.

Leading well begins with what we think and what we say. Our attitude is extremely important if we desire to lead others.

In the church we don't make widgets; we don't provide a

service. We have only one product: Relationship. We offer a relationship with the Creator and a relationship with other believers. Attitudes can make or break those relationships.

As ministry leaders, we have to be careful and mindful of our internal thoughts. They come out in our attitudes and our actions. One moment of weakness, one second of letting our mouth run wild, one outburst of anger can sabotage a relationship or an entire ministry. That doesn't seem fair, but it's true.

We have to understand that we have a higher level of accountability for what we do. Sin is sin for a leader or a follower. Even though people often try to hold their leaders to a higher standard of righteousness, there isn't one. What's right for one is right for the other. What's wrong for one is wrong for the other.

But even though there's only one standard for all people regarding sin, responsibility and accountability are greater for a leader than for a regular person. As a Second Mile Leader, you are going to step into an area of greater accountability for your actions than other people you are leading. This is a hard truth to come to terms with. And it's why James says the following:

> *Dear brothers and sisters, not many of you should become teachers in the church, for **we who teach will be judged more strictly**. Indeed, we all make many mistakes. For if we could control our tongues, we would be perfect and could also control ourselves in every other way. We can make a large horse go wherever we want by means of a small bit in its mouth. And a small rudder*

*makes a huge ship turn wherever the pilot chooses to go,
even though the winds are strong. In the same way, the
tongue is a small thing that makes grand speeches. But
a tiny spark can set a great forest on fire. (James 3:1-5
NLT)*

James gives a warning for those who would be teachers and leaders. There will be a stricter judgement for us. People trust us for direction from God. As leaders, whatever direction we set the people will follow.

Notice the language of the remainder of the passage in James. It's leadership language. The rider bridles the horse; the captain steers the the ship; the arsonist is responsible for the forest burning. Even though the example of taming the tongue applies to every member of the church, James is speaking to teachers and leaders. It's important to remember that what we say can direct the whole ship, the whole church, or the whole ministry.

As a leader, we must remember that we carry tremendous power in our words. This is why we see such tremendous consequences for leaders in scripture when they were disobedient to God. Saul was stripped of his kingdom. David's son died. Moses was prohibited from entering the promised land. Top leaders faced severe consequences for disobedience. Leaders' decisions to obey or rebel encourage obedience or embolden rebellion in the people we lead.

James acknowledges that we all make mistakes. We all have bad days. We say stupid things. But he does it in a context that prompts us to remember: When we aren't feeling well, when we are grumpy, when we are dealing with anger or bitterness, what we say and how we act in the moment could have permanent effects. As leaders, when we're having a bad day, sometimes it's best just to keep our mouths shut.

**A bad attitude will destroy our influence;
a good one will expand it.**

There is a powerful story about attitude in 1 Samuel 25. David is still on the run from King Saul, so he's having to depend on the kindness of strangers. He hears about a man named Nabal who is wealthy and asks for his assistance. The Bible describes Nabal as "crude and mean in all his dealings" (1 Samuel 25:3 NLT). What happens next reveals Nabal's attitude and sets him on a collision course for death.

David's request for assistance is denied–harshly. Nabal's response to David's messengers reveals that he has a proud heart about his own achievements and scorn for David. Nabal doesn't understand why someone as lowly as David would come and request a self-made man like himself to give him *anything*. Here's his response:

"Who is this fellow David?" Nabal sneered to the young men. "Who does this son of Jesse think he is? There are lots of servants these days who run away from their masters. Should I take my bread and my water and my meat that I've slaughtered for my shearers and give it to a band of outlaws who come from who knows where?" (1

Samuel 25:10-11 NLT)

Nabal has serious lapse in judgement. No one tells him, "You better watch your attitude!" His low opinion of David and high opinion of himself causes him to make statements that will cost him his life. His attitude becomes the death of him.

He doesn't take the time to consider who David is or where he is headed. He doesn't realize his contempt is about to rouse the fury of the future king of Israel. He has no idea that David has 600 warriors that can take what they want–especially after they are insulted.

David is enraged by the contempt his has been shown. 1 Samuel 25:13 says, "'Get your swords!' was David's reply as he strapped on his own."

We have to watch our attitudes. They can get us into serious trouble. For us it could just spell the end of our leadership or ministry, but for Nabal it spelled the end of his life.

In contrast to Nabal, Abigail, his wife, was wise and gracious. As soon as she heard what had happened, she ran to meet David and plead for mercy. She repented on behalf of Nabal for his attitude.

When Abigail saw David, she quickly got off her donkey and bowed low before him. She fell at his feet and said, "I accept all blame in this matter, my lord. Please listen to what I have to say. I know Nabal is a wicked and ill-tempered man; please don't pay any attention to him. He is a fool, just as his name suggests. But I nev-

er even saw the young men you sent. "Now, my lord, as surely as the LORD lives and you yourself live, since the LORD has kept you from murdering and taking vengeance into your own hands, let all your enemies and those who try to harm you be as cursed as Nabal is. (1 Samuel 25:23-26 NLT)

Notice Abigail's description of her husband. She says he is ill-tempered–a man with a bad attitude. She describes him as cursed.

We can't afford for these descriptions to be given about us as we attempt to influence others in the kingdom. Our attitudes can bring blessing or curses on us.

Abigail's attitude of humility saved her household and even temporarily spared her horrible husband's life. David told her, *"Return home in peace. I have heard what you said. We will not kill your husband." (1 Samuel 25:35 NLT).*

This is a question to ponder: Are we needing to be saved by people around us because of our bad attitudes or are we saving people around us because of our good ones?

We shouldn't treat people with contempt but with concern.

Bad attitudes will always lead to the end of something–a relationship, a job, or even our lives. We have to watch our attitudes as my mom used to say. A bad attitude will destroy our influence; a good one will expand it.

Contempt is an attitude Nabal displayed that leaders should

avoid. He regarded David as a little guy, perhaps even a runaway slave. Although David had the potential to destroy Nabal, his own arrogance led him into a blind belief that David posed no threat to his existence.

As a leader there will be many people God places in our path who seem that they may be undeserving of our attention. Without a proper understanding of God's grace in our life along with the role of a leader, we will treat people with the same contempt Nabal showed David.

Remember that none of us deserve what we have received from God. We are who and what we are because of his intervention in our lives. Further, it is our role and responsibility to become God's intervention in the lives of others; therefore, we shouldn't treat people with contempt but with concern. God has placed them in our life and path for us to minister to them and demonstrate His grace.

Treating people with contempt doesn't go well in the business world or society. We are not very likeable when our attitudes and egos are inflated. No one wants to be around us. Our leadership influence diminishes, and we find ourselves surrounded by the only person we hold in high esteem: Ourselves.

There are also consequences to having this view of others. The Bible tells us that God Himself defends the marginalized and the underprivileged. He takes up the cause of those who are oppressed by pompous, powerful people. If we allow the attitude of contempt to sneak into our hearts, we might just find God Himself working against us as He works for those who are dear to His heart.

It's wisdom to have a healthy view of people that doesn't

cause us to treat them as less than we are. As the old saying goes, "Be kind to everyone on the way up; you'll meet the same people on the way down."

A lack of gratitude in our attitude will keep humility far from us.

Perhaps the reason Nabal displayed the attitude of contempt toward David is because of the attitude he had toward himself. Nabal had an inflated opinion of himself. His self-admiration was out of control.

When we develop an inflated opinion of ourselves, it leads to us treating others with contempt. What is the root of having such a high opinion? It's complete disregard for God's role in our lives.

When we begin to believe we are self-made, we have little patience for other people in our lives. We think we pulled ourselves up by our own bootstraps. Since we conquered our issues, others should be able to do the same. We think or even say, "Get over it!"

We believe we did it all ourselves, so we are ungrateful. A lack of gratitude in our attitude will keep humility far from us. We will see ourselves as the source of every blessing. We will have zero tolerance for people who can't go and obtain their own.

Guard Your Attitude

Our role as leaders is to build people. Honestly it's exhausting. In spite of our best efforts, many people never "get it." They never grow up and take the next step in their lives no matter how many times you explain it or demonstrate it.

And so we run out of patience. We think that because *we* believe they should have gotten it by now they no longer deserve our assistance. We've shown them the ropes. Now it's up to them. They need to get over their issues. If they want to climb out of their situation, they can do just like we had to do. We'll be right over here waiting whenever they do.

Be careful of letting this attitude slip into your life and ministry. It will do its best to slip in when people leave your area of ministry after you've been there for them, answered their phone calls, spent time encouraging them, prayed with them, and trained them. And they still leave. Sometimes they may even blame you for letting them down when you've been through it all right beside them. That hurts. But don't allow it to sour your attitude. Be grateful for God's grace in allowing you to serve in leadership.

Nabal's attitude worked its way out in his words and deeds. Having allowed his scornful thoughts to consume him, he now blurts out several sentences that pronounce judgement on David. The pronouncements actually become a curse on his own life. Be careful of what you allow to come out of your mouth. Our words can get us into awkward situations and hot water.

Years ago Aimee's brother Steve was getting married. We went to the airport to pick up one of his friends, Les, who flew in to be in his wedding. Aimee and I were dating, and at the time our relationship was somewhat controversial. I am five years older than Aimee, so not everyone was as thrilled about our relationship as we were.

Les and I met for the first time at the airport. The extent of our relationship at that point was each other's names. As we were driving back from the airport, Les and Aimee's other brother, Chris, were sitting in the front seat chatting. I was sitting in the back seat listening to them catch up on the latest happenings of their lives. Suddenly Les turned to Chris and said, "So who's this jerk who's dating your sister?" If ever there were a perfect time to utter the phrase, "Well, this is awkward," that was it.

Chris cavalierly gestured with this thumb toward me in the backseat and said, "Him." The awkward tension was immediately palpable. For a couple of moments no one said anything. We were at the awkward showdown. Then Les turned awkwardly to me and forced out, "Oh, hey, dude!" It was very awkward for Les and me. Chris, however, thought it was absolutely hilarious.

Getting Into Hot Water

Our mouths can get us into trouble when we don't realize the context of our situation. I've done this many times, and I've watched others do it to themselves. I much prefer the latter. When I'm not the one creating the awkward situation, it's hilarious to watch. I've watched people speak their minds when they should just keep their opinions to themselves. I've seen people fail to know their audience before they speak. They introduce controversial topics or start political conversations without recognizing who's in the room. It's awkward and hilarious to watch.

When it's accidental, it is usually just awkward; people laugh and awkwardly apologize. Everyone moves on. But when it comes from a bad attitude and a heart filled with malice, it's not funny. It's offensive and polarizing. People withdraw from relationship and away from our potential leadership.

Nabal had a bad attitude. He failed to evaluate his context. He didn't realize he was addressing the King. His wife saved the household with her humility. If Nabal had simply chosen kindness and humility as a way of life, her intervention would have been unnecessary.

Our attitude toward people should be that they are important. Treat everyone as important and you'll never have to worry as to whether they are. After all, people don't get their value from their positions, possessions, or popularity. They get it from their creator, and He values everyone–rich, poor, famous, and obscure. Even if they aren't important to you, they are important to Him.

Nabal's arrogant words brought his whole house under threat of death. This brings us full circle to the caution James had for us: Our tongue speaks under the influence of our attitude. It has the power to steer an entire ship with everyone on it. It has the ability to burn down a whole forest and devastate every living thing.

As a leader our attitude is infectious. People will watch and listen to us. They will emulate our actions and take their cues from our attitudes. We have the power to lead them into blessing or curses. This is a tremendous responsibility and one we must never forget. A bad attitude will eventually catch up with us–in the worst of ways, in the worst of times. We must guard our attitudes. As my mom used to say, "You better watch your attitude!" You as a leader lead people into consequences.

Good or bad, you are responsible for them.

Attitude Adjustment

If our attitudes need adjusting, we can get them realigned easily. They improve as our minds are renewed. Ephesians says that as we grow close to Christ, our attitudes begin to reflect His.

> *Since you have heard about Jesus and have learned the truth that comes from him, throw off your old sinful nature and your former way of life, which is corrupted by lust and deception. Instead, **let the Spirit renew your thoughts and attitudes**.*
> *(Ephesians 4:21-23 NLT)*

If our attitudes aren't right, we need to check the amount of time we are spending in devotion. All of us have 24 hours in a day. Many of us allow God to slip to the last thing we do rather than the first thing we do. The more we are with God, the more we will be like Him. The more we are distant from Him, the less our attitudes will reflect His.

We also have control over our attitudes because we have control over our thoughts. Second Corinthians 10:5 says, *"[W]e take captive every thought to make it obedient to Christ."*

Attitudes are like an emotional thermometer. Our emotional state is largely driven by our thought life. We can control what we think about, and our attitudes will reflect the emotional change.

Don't simply let your emotional state rule you. Take control of your thoughts. We can't stop thinking, but we can change what we think about.

> *And now, dear brothers and sisters, one final thing.* **Fix** *your thoughts on what is true, and honorable, and right, and pure, and lovely, and admirable. Think about things that are excellent and worthy of praise. (Phillipians 4:8 NLT)*

Notice we are to *fix* out thoughts. This means to focus them on, but the play on words works as well. We need our thinking fixed. For many of us, it's broken. If we can fix our thoughts, we can fix our attitudes. If we think about the things this verse says to think about, we will have much better attitudes. We can get a better attitude when we choose it.

**Whatever attitude we take into the situation
is a pretty good indicator of how it will turn out.**

Our Attitude Determines Our Altitude

Zig Ziglar said that your attitude, not your aptitude, will determine your altitude. The thing that will limit or lift your potential more than anything else is your attitude. Most of us think that it's our skills, techniques, and abilities that make us great leaders; however, we really begin to lead and influence people when we have right attitudes about our situation and ourselves.

A plane with its nose pointed down is headed toward the ground. If a pilot desires for his plane to gain altitude, he has to apply power and lift the nose up toward the sky. The position of the nose is called the plane's attitude.

Have you seen people who are always down? These people walk around with a sour attitude. They bring themselves and everyone around them down. Others don't like to be around people with a bad attitude. Be a person who's looking up. Be a person who's looking over the circumstances for a solution. Find ways to improve the situation and lift the spirits of everyone around you. You'll go further than those who are always looking down. If you want to go higher, adjust your attitude!

Our Attitude Predicts Success Or Failure

In so many situations the battle is won before it has begun. It all has to do with the frame of mind with which we enter the battle. Are we full of faith, hope, and optimism, or are we negative and doubtful of getting results?

If we don't correct our attitudes, it is highly likely that the negative outcome we expect will become a reality. When we believe we're going to fail, we make only half-hearted attempts or no effort at all. By our inaction, the outcome is assured. Whatever attitude we take into the situation is a pretty good indicator of how it will turn out. Henry Ford said it like this, "Whether a man thinks he can or he can't, he's right!"

I played basketball in high school. Our record was abysmal. We won only a handful of games over three years. Our team was made up of several guys who played street ball together all the time. We were excellent when we were just playing for fun. But somehow, when we took the court in the gym, we lost almost every game. If you had asked any of our team what we expected the outcome of our game to be, I can assure you nearly everyone expected us to lose. The outcome of the game was determined before we ever left the locker room.

We have to get rid of negative attitudes in our minds if we are to be successful at leading others. For every person who finds a way to lose when everything is in his favor, there is someone else who finds a way to win in spite of his circumstances. The difference maker isn't skill, tools, or resources. It's attitude.

Good people won't follow leaders with bad attitudes.

Our Attitude Sets the Atmosphere

Generally speaking, people are thermometers. They adjust to the temperature of the room. But leaders aren't thermometers; leaders are thermostats. Sure, they *have* a thermometer. They can read the room. They understand what is going on when they walk in. The difference is leaders do something about it. They take responsibility for the room. They set the temperature in the room to what *they* want it to be.

If you want the climate of the room to be happiness, fill it with happiness. If you want your team to be grateful, be grateful. If you want the atmosphere to be friendly, be friendly.

It's the law of sowing and reaping.

Give, and it will be given to you. (Luke 6:38 NIV)

You will always harvest what you plant. (Galatians 6:7 NLT)

Just as you can change the temperature of a room, you can change the culture of the teams you lead. If you want belief, sow belief. If you want trust, be trusting. If you want positive attitudes, be optimistic.

If we are always negative, saying how people are unfaithful, unreliable, bad, and faulty, those are the only people you will have. The others will find another leader or boss. So the words we speak will become truth. Good people won't follow leaders with bad attitudes.

If you'd love to have a great day at work, walk into the room cheerfully, smiling, laughing, and complimenting people. Tell them how amazing they are, how thankful you are to have them in your life, and how you can't wait to see what happens today. Their response will amaze you as they reflect your attitude back to you. Leaders know they specialize in climate control. They use their attitude to adjust the atmosphere.

Our Attitude Turns Problems Into Possibilities

We can wallow in discouragement or begin to dream. We can blame or build. We can get angry or take action. We can concede or conquer. It's up to us whether we remain stuck in our problem or turn it into a possibility. God can take any problem and turn it into a possibility:

> *And we know that God causes everything to work together for the good of those who love God and are called according to his purpose for them. (Romans 8:28 NLT)*

Think of how much of the Bible was written by prisoners, oppressed people, and those in captivity. Paul turned his beatings and imprisonments into opportunities to write letters to the churches he started. If they can win in those circumstances, so can we.

> *"Everything is possible to him that believes." (Mark 9:23 NIV)*

There's a story about two shoe salesmen. They both encountered the same situation. One could see only the problem. The other saw the possibility.

A shoe salesman was sent to a faraway country, and after a few days he sent back the message, "Coming home; nobody wears shoes here." Another salesman from the shoe company visited the same country. He wrote back to the home office after a few days: "Send more shoes! Nobody over here has them yet!"

Two people saw the same situation with a different set of eyes. When you think about the team you lead, you can think, "Nobody serves here. I can't succeed," or "Nobody serves here, yet. I have an unlimited potential with this team."

We will fix our happiness when we change our attitude.

Our Attitude Determines Our Happiness

It's not what we accomplish that makes us happy. It's the way we *view* what we do that makes us happy. Many of us spend our time and effort chasing a finish line that is elusive or perhaps an illusion altogether.

Some people can't celebrate any accomplishment. As soon as they do something great, they move the finish line further away. Their lives are filled with insecurity and frustration. There is no gratitude in their lives. A person like this will never be happy in spite of the fact that they are an incredible success. Solomon was an example of this. Even though he was incredibly wise and successful, he lost the meaning of life in all his achievements.

> But as I looked at everything I had worked so hard to accomplish, it was all so meaningless—like chasing the wind. There was nothing really worthwhile anywhere. (Ecclesiastes 2:11 (NLT)

If Solomon was susceptible, we can be also. Every time we have a negative attitude about our problems and issues we have in our lives, we really should take a moment to express gratitude. Regardless of the issues we are facing, it's highly likely that somewhere someone in the world would love to trade places with us. I once heard someone say, "There are millions of people who would love to have my problems." Thinking of that humbling statement will change your attitude quickly.

> *So I concluded there is nothing better than to be happy and enjoy ourselves as long as we can. And people should eat and drink and enjoy the fruits of their labor, for these are gifts from God. (Ecclesiastes 3:12-13 NLT)*

We have to change our attitudes about our work and our accomplishments. It's the journey, not the destination that's important. Enjoy working through the problems. It's all part of the process. God wants us to enjoy the process and to allow Him to participate in it with us.

John Maxwell said it like this, "The thoughts in your mind are more important than the things in your life." Too many leaders think if they could just move to a new place or have different circumstances, then they would be happy. This isn't true. There's a saying that reveals the problem, "Everywhere I go, there I am!" We will fix our happiness when we change our attitude.

Attitude Adjustment Advised

All of us fall into the trap of bad attitudes, some of us more than others. We need continual adjustment and correction. That's OK. The problem occurs when we stop making the adjustments and let our attitudes run our lives into a ditch.

If you ever drive a car down the highway, you know that it takes continuous input and adjustment to keep it on the road. If you just let go of the wheel and assume it will stay in its lane, you'll probably end up with a trip to the hospital fairly soon. Keep adjusting. Below are some indicators that your attitude might need some attention:

- I have strained relationships.
- I have a low view of people.
- I have a cynical perspective.
- I am discouraged.
- I think more about how good yesterday was than how good tomorrow can be.
- I have no drive.

If any of these are true, it's probably time to pull back from relationships, get alone with God, and take inventory of His blessings in your life.

As you're becoming a leader in your church, here are some things to ask yourself regarding your attitude:

- How do I respond when asked to do something new or outside my comfort zone?
- How do I respond when I'm inconvenienced?
- If people hung out with me, would they catch positive attitudes?
- Would they be encouraged or discouraged?

- What is at the root of negative attitudes and how can we combat those?

As we move into leadership, we must be vigilant constantly about our attitude and perspective. It's contagious. As leaders, people will do what they see us do; therefore it's important to remember to

WATCH YOUR ATTITUDE!

11

MAKING DISCIPLES

Go and make disciples. Teach these new disciples to obey all
the commands I have given you.
- Jesus (Matthew 28:-19-20 NLT)

One of my jobs before I went on staff at the church for the first time was as a laborer and finisher for a concrete company in Russellville, Arkansas. It was a difficult yet rewarding job. You could look back at the end of the day and see all that you had accomplished.

One particular day when I went to work, we were pouring a driveway apron that tapered from the road to the main part of the drive. Part of my job was to help shape and finish the rounded part of the curb. I was having a difficult time. Every time I would bring the trowel down the curb, I would make the concrete look pretty good. Yet on my second pass back up the slope of the curb, my trowel would gouge out a chunk of concrete just about every time. I was getting extremely frustrated.

Adding to my frustration that day was the heat. In Arkansas the temperature and humidity can combine to make some pretty miserable working conditions. That day they were both high. It was horrible. But there was something that made that particular day really bad. The day before, Aimee had broken up with me. I was not coping well with the uncooperative concrete, the stifling temperatures, and my broken heart. I was struggling to concentrate and keep my emotions in check.

My boss, Danny Taylor, was giving me a hard time. We always poked fun at one another as often as possible, so he was heckling me as I was struggling to finish the curb. My cousin, Jerry, worked at the same company. He decided to try to help me out by informing Danny about my current relationship status—"single"—thinking Danny would relent and have some compassion.

Oh, no! This was merely fuel on the fire. Danny decided this was a great opportunity to harass me even more. At one point, when all my frustration boiled over, he jabbed with one last statement, "It's just a job, Jon!" He laughed, knowing I was fuming, but insinuating that I should be able to calm myself regardless of all that was going on. He was having fun at my expense. I was having no fun whatsoever.

A couple of days later we were pouring the drainage basin at the bottom of this same driveway project. Storm clouds began to gather just as the concrete truck arrived. I did my best to talk Danny out of pouring this section of driveway since every drop of rain that fell would find its way right to where we were working. Wanting to hurry and complete the job, Danny made the decision to pour the concrete anyway. No sooner had we poured and begun finishing the concrete, the bottom fell out of the sky. The rain came. Torrential rain.

Water was running over our freshly poured concrete, washing everything away as we frantically tried to figure out a way to cover it with plastic and divert the water. Danny was extremely frustrated with our situation. The concrete was ruined. The pour was wasted. We would have to break up the concrete once it cured and start all over again. I realized Danny was extremely upset about what had just happened, so I knew this was my moment for vengeance. Walking up to him and clapping him on the shoulder, I grinned and said, "It's just a job, Danny."

His eyes met mine. He was fuming. Then a look of recognition as he realized that I had just been able to exact my revenge on him. We both broke out into laughter. We laughed a lot. It was a great "touché" moment for me. Score one for Jon. We were even.

I really enjoyed working for Doug and Danny Taylor most days. The work was hard but rewarding. There was only one problem—I never got any better at finishing concrete. I was terrific at setting forms, cutting wire, washing tools, and running wheelbarrows full of concrete, but we weren't a company that just *poured* concrete, we were concrete *finishers*. And I couldn't seem to get that part right.

This makes me think of the church. We have a specific task that we are responsible to accomplish. We do lots of activities. Our calendars are full. We are certainly busy, but are we doing the one that that we are supposed to be accomplishing?

Jesus didn't tell us simply to teach. He said teach to obey.

Make Disciples

Jesus made this one objective clear before He left the planet. In his final instructions, he said

*Go and **make disciples** of all the nations, baptizing them in the name of the Father and the Son and the Holy Spirit. Teach these new disciples to obey all the commands I have given you. (Matthew 28:-19-20 NLT)*

The mission could not be clearer. We are to make disciples. Jesus didn't say make converts. He didn't say conduct weekend services and revivals. He didn't say fill your calendars with tons of activities to draw people to your church. While some of those things may be the tools, they aren't the mission of the church.

The mission is clear: make disciples. Jesus then clarifies what it means to make a disciple in verse 20–**teach to obey all**. This is the simple explanation of what it means to help disciple someone. We are to teach them to obey all things Jesus commanded.

The church is great at teaching. People love to come to the church services and hear someone tell them something they never knew before. They love to have the "wow" factor in the teaching. They are impressed when we can explain why a verse was written the way it was or why that Greek word is important or why Paul used a particular phrase and what it meant to his audience.

The problem is that many people love to be wowed but do not love to be obedient. Jesus didn't tell us simply to teach. He said teach to obey. Many people have been taught God's word but never taught to obey His word. For this reason, many in the church *age* but never *mature*. They grow *old* in Christ, but they never grow *up*.

We are commanded in scripture to be more than hearers of the word; we are to be doers. We have to teach people for more than just information. We have to teach for transformation. Sadly many never move past the prayer of salvation. They make a verbal affirmation that they would love to have Jesus as their Savior, but they never make him their Lord. It doesn't work like that.

Jesus says to obey not *part* but *all* the things He commanded. We are not allowed to use our own discretion to pick and choose which portions of Jesus' teachings we obey. We don't get to take the parts we love and leave the parts we hate. It's all or nothing with Jesus. He doesn't take partial commitments or obedience. We are commanded to become fully obedient followers of all His teachings. To stop short of this is to make converts, not disciples. It's like me knowing how to pour concrete but never getting good at making the final product. As Second Mile Leaders, if we stop short of making disciples, we aren't really doing what Jesus left us here to do.

Becoming fully obedient doesn't happen overnight. It's a lifelong process. In fact there are things that Jesus will be working on in our lives to complete His work until we draw our last breath or until He returns. But even if Jesus' work in us is slow, it should never come to a standstill.

As leaders we are to *become* disciples who *make* disciples. The work of God should be progressing in our lives as we help it move forward in the lives of those around us.

As Second Mile Leaders, we realize the purpose of our lives

here on this Earth is to see Jesus fully formed in the lives of those around us. We are disciples who make disciples that make disciples.

**We all need others to help us complete
the discipleship process in our lives.**

Next Steps

Disciples are not manufactured through our Sunday services. They are matured in relationships. We need to do more than sit in rows on Sundays; we need to sit in circles throughout the week. Disciple making is best done face-to-face and life-on-life over a long period of time.

When people raise their hand or come forward to accept Christ as Savior, they are taking the *first* step in a lifelong journey of following Jesus. They need help to take their next steps. Those steps are coached and encouraged by spiritual mentors and leaders in their lives.

Spiritual babies need nurturing and care if Christ is ever to be formed fully in them. To stop short of providing these nurturing relationships is spiritual abandonment. Discipleship happens through consistent, committed relationships between the new believer and a leader/mentor in the believer's life.

It is not just new believers who need to take next steps in their discipleship process, it's *all* believers. Churches are full of people who love God but are not yet fully obedient to Christ. We *all* need others to help us complete the discipleship process in our lives.

When we have someone with whom we can be real about the struggles we have, we are able to walk together in accountability as we take our next steps of obedience to Christ.

Grow People

An old Chinese proverb says, "If you want 1 year of prosperity, grow grain. If you want 10 years of prosperity, grow trees. If you want 100 years of prosperity, grow people." Making disciples is growing people, and it's the most worthwhile investment and purpose for our lives.

As a Second Mile Leader, God has you in the lives of others to influence them for His purpose and desires in their lives. This is going to require you to be consistent, faithful, trustworthy, and diligent–for a long time. As you do this, you'll have the joy of seeing people take next steps in their walk with God. There is nothing more rewarding.

Relationships like this don't happen accidentally. They require lots of intentional pursuit. To this point, your pursuit of relationships may have been passive. Your position may have been "If they want to know me, they can." Now, as a Second Mile Leader, you will be required to pursue intentionally those relationships that facilitate discipleship. For the next portion of this chapter, we will focus on three things you must do well to begin and build the type of relationships that give you the opportunity to speak into the lives of people around you: connect, serve, and influence.

**If you want to be a person who is able to
connect with people, you have to be real.**

Connect

Our church is made up of small groups. This is where we believe that discipleship happens best. With every new season of groups, new group leaders come to speak with me about how to get people to sign up for their group. The lack of registration from their group is an obvious indicator that they have few connections with others. They hope that people will pursue them. It doesn't happen. Their groups never fill up and the leader becomes discouraged. As a leader, it is imperative to embrace this idea: Leaders must connect with others.

When I was growing up, I was extremely shy. I attended a church for two solid years without making a single friend. Then one Sunday, two girls from the youth group took the initiative to invite me to be a part of the youth group. That invitation shaped my life and my destiny. Truthfully I don't know that I would be in ministry had they not invited me to attend the youth group.

Most people now think that I'm one of the most outgoing people in the world, but that's not true. The difference is that I have learned some basic skills about how to connect with people. I credit a book written by Dale Carnegie, *How To Win Friends and Influence People*, as one of the most influential books I've ever read. It gave me the tools and resources to be able to cultivate and create relationships with people that I did not know.

One of the first principles in Dale's classic book is simply to develop a genuine interest in people. This is key if you're going to be successful at connecting and discipling others.

The great part about being sincerely interested in others is that a lot of the effort of the conversation and relationship is off your shoulders; for example, I can listen to men talk about their work, their systems, and the tools they use for endless hours of conversation.

I have deep concern and empathy for people as they go through emotional struggles of life. I can sit across from a married couple as they pour out their hearts about the struggles that they're having in their marriage or with their children. Most of the time, I do little of the talking. I just listen. It is my genuine interest in people coupled with a few tidbits of wisdom that I offer at some point in the conversation that gives me influence. It is how I connect.

People love to talk about themselves, so all I really have to do is prompt them to continue sharing their life, their hopes, and their dreams. They are more than willing to share, and a deep connection develops. Many people leave conversations with me with a deep sense of connection. The secret is that it's not because of how much I said, but because of how much I listened.

Connection with people happens only when we demonstrate genuine concern and care. We must be about them and not ourselves. It's been said many times this way: "People don't care how much you know until they know how much you care." Connecting with people is easy as long as we follow some basic principles.

Be Real

It's amazing to me how people's language changes immediately upon entering a church facility. Normal conversation turns to Christian colloquialisms and religious jargon. It's as though they forget how to be regular people when they show up to church. They use this "face" to hide. They sound religious, but they aren't real.

If you want to be a person who is able to connect with people, you have to be real. People spot a phony a mile away. Fake is disconnecting because it undermines trust. If you can't be who you really are, the other person picks up the cue that they shouldn't reveal who they are either.

In my previous church, we tried very hard to reconnect people who had left the church. A common reason they often gave for leaving the church was that "the church is full of hypocrites." Their perspective was that the church is a place for people to pretend to be something on Sunday that they can't back up the rest of the week, and they wanted nothing to do with it.

Fake isn't just about pretending to be something we're not. It's also failing to live what we proclaim we believe. This is the other part of real–we have to practice what we preach. If we say one thing and do another, it reduces our credibility. People don't like to connect with others who can't be trusted.

If you've got issues, be real about them. You don't have to air your dirty laundry to every person that you come into contact with, but don't pretend to be something that you're not. Putting on airs or acting holy when you're just a regular ol' Joe is off-putting, and people don't like it. Be real. Communicate with openness and sincerity. Don't try to impress people with religious speak and hyper-spiritual language. Just be you.

Be Interested

God gave us two ears and one mouth. That's a pretty big clue. That means two-thirds of the time should be spent listening and only one-third speaking. As I said before, one of the reasons that I'm able to connect with people so well is that I simply shut up and listen.

Many people, because of their own insecurities or pride, want to do all the talking. The persons they find most interesting are themselves. They don't listen when others speak; instead they use the break to take a breath and prepare their next verbal barrage.

This communicates a big idea to people: You don't matter. If you want to be someone who draws people into authentic and genuine relationship, you have to be interested in them, not just yourself.

Being interested means you value the person you're trying to connect with. You need to get to know them. This means knowing their name, listening to their stories, and learning their dreams. When you do, speak in terms of things *they* find interesting, not in terms of things that interest only you.

Be Intentional

Most great things don't happen by accident. Relationships are no different. One of the things that bugs me is when people say, "We should get together sometime." While this statement may express a heartfelt desire to connect, there is no accompanying intentional commitment. The result is that few of these sentiments ever materialize into subsequent meetings and relational development.

It's better to say, "Let's get together Tuesday at 7 p.m." If you do this, the meeting is much more likely to happen because there is intentionality with this statement. This is pursuit of relationship.

Leaders know they must have intentional initiative. They have to be the one who sends the text message, makes the phone call, or arranges the meeting. Leaders know that they have to move to where people are, literally and figuratively. They have to make the drive, take the trip. They also have to learn the culture of the people they desire to reach.

Often things that are norms for our church culture are not normal for the people that we are trying to reach. While our goal may be to move them toward our culture, we need to adapt to others instead of expecting them to adapt to us. Our goal is to walk in their shoes, not get them to walk in ours.

**We have to look past what people are
to see what they can become.**

Believe In Them

All people matter to God, but if we're honest, not everyone matters to us. This sobering reality is something we need God to change in our hearts. We need Him to give us a love to see people as He sees them, not as we see them. From the person that is our closest friend to our worst enemy, or from the person that has the most to offer to the least of these, everyone is valuable to God. He created us all. Many of his children are wayward and lost. He desires for us to love as he loves.

We need to see as Jesus sees in order to love as He loves. People know when we're being sincere and when we're just faking It. It's one thing to communicate to people because you believe you have something of value to say. It's another to communicate with people because you believe they have value.

Not only do we need to be able to see their intrinsic value, we need to be able to see their potential. We have to look past what people are to see what they can become. Then we can inspire them to become all that God says they can be.

Be Their Cheerleader

People need hope. Many are struggling under loads that are more than they can carry. As a result, they are ready to give up and quit. They need someone to come along and give them a breath of fresh air, to put wind in their sails, to help them believe they can make it.

Jeremiah 29:11 says, "For I know the plans I have for you," declares the Lord, "plans to prosper you and not to harm you, plans to give you hope and a future." Without hope we will never see our future. God desires for us to live in hope. We as leaders need to be able to dispense hope. Our presence and our words should lift the spirits of those around us to believe that tomorrow doesn't have to be like today.

French general Napoleon Bonaparte said, "Leaders are dealers in hope." When you give people hope, they can believe again for a better future. When you give people hope, people want to be near you, not for what they see in you, but for what you see in them.

The true goal of a leader is to develop the God-given talents and destinies in the lives of those around you.

Be Persistent

It can be difficult to cultivate relationships with people. When we reach out to connect, we will usually run into some type of obstacle. Many times people will decline our initial or even subsequent attempts to get together and connect.

There may be legitimate reasons for this. With full calendars, it's difficult for all of us to add something to the mix, and this new relationship you're trying to form is, after all, new. Knowing this, we need to be prepared for it to take a few tries to get together.

Sometimes their reasons are simply smokescreens. The person you're trying to connect with might have a history of failed relationships. They might also have the experience that people want to get together only for what they can take from the relationship, not what they can give.

Others may simply be testing you. They may try to hold you at arm's length to see if you're willing to persist. They may be checking to see if you're one of those people who has abandoned them in the past when things got tough. Either way, your persistence and consideration will open the door. Keep pushing. Gently.

Keep in mind that as leaders we must always be the initiator. We are not waiting for people to connect with us. We are wanting to connect with them. Take the first step with others, and then make the effort to continue building relationships.

Be Consistent

Jesus was able to see such radical transformation in his disciples because of the consistency of his interactions with them. They had daily interaction with Jesus for 3½ years. That type of proximity and consistency develops deep, lasting, and trusting relationships.

Not many of us are going to move in with another family or have them move in with us, but we can be intentional about creating regular encounters and conversations. Plan your next outing while you're still together for the first one. That way it's already on the books and less likely to get bumped. Intentional, consistent pursuit of the relationship will help it grow past the polite and pleasant platitudes of shallow relationships and into more meaningful conversations about things that really matter.

SERVE

I remember a few years ago reflecting deeply on my life's purpose and meaning. I imagined my funeral and what I would like people to say about me when I was lying in the casket at the front of the church. As I considered what I would like to be said, a common theme emerged. I hoped each person would say their life was better because I was in it. I helped them. I served them. Some part of their life was saved or restored because of something I did. Their lives were better because I shared mine with them.

Working backward from this ending ceremony of my life, I asked a simple question: What could I do *now* that would make them say those words *then*? The simple answer was that I should live to add value to the people around me. I should work hard to make sure that every contact I had with people somehow enriched their lives.

I decided that I would work to become a resource for other people. If their marriage was in trouble, I would offer my own advice and experience on marriage. If there was another situation they faced for which I had no reference, knowledge, or experience, I would obtain it. I would read a book or watch a video to learn something to help them. For the most part, this is what I've done. I do my best to grow so that I can give what I know. We add value by serving others.

Many people view leadership through the lens of *personal* success. They leverage others' time, talents, and energy to propel them to the top of the corporate ladder. They stand on the shoulders of others as they advance their own agenda. Few of those who view leadership this way make it very far. Only those who learn to leverage their lives to develop others really have the social equity to make it to the top.

The more people you serve the more successful you will be.

Your true goal as a leader is to develop the God-given talents and destinies in the lives of those around you. Learn where the people you serve are wanting to go and help them get there. Leadership is easier when you're helping people go the way they are made to go.

All relationships either add to or subtract from a person's life. You know this. It's likely you have some people in your life that you dread speaking to. You may even ignore their phone call when it comes. It would be good to ask the question of yourself, "Am I the type of person that people love to talk to or the one they avoid? Do they walk away from our interactions with more strength, energy, and courage or do they walk away feeling I have drained the life out of them?"

Jesus told us the secret to success. He said the greatest will be the servant. The top leader is the top server. If you want to make a big impact in this world, you have to find a way to serve. The more people you serve, the more successful you will be. It's been said that "Leadership isn't how far we advance ourselves but how far we advance others."

Leaders are life givers through their service to others. How are you making things better for the people around you?

INFLUENCE

It's been said that the true measure of leadership is influence. If we have no influence, we have no leadership. Many people have the title of a leader, but if they have no one following them or changing because of their influence, they really aren't leading at all.

John Maxwell says it like this: "He that thinketh he leadeth and hath no one following him is only taking a walk." Without anyone implementing our recommendations, learning from us, or emulating our behaviors, we have no influence. Paul said it like this: "Follow me *as* I follow Christ." Follow my example. Let me get close enough to you that you can see my life and lifestyle and you'll follow it.

We cannot make disciples without influence. Our leadership influence will grow when we have connected and then served. Only after we have added value to the lives of those around us will they entertain our ideas about how to live life according to our paradigm. This is when our leadership begins. This is when we can begin to make a disciple.

When we gain influence, we must leverage it for the purpose God has given it to us. If we abuse our leadership to manipulate or make people serve our interests, we will break trust with the people we have the opportunity to lead, and our influence will be gone. We must lead for a cause that is beyond us. We must lead people into a vision that is bigger than their own self-interests.

We are accountable to God for how we use our influence. Our goal is to make disciples, teaching them to obey all that Jesus commanded. That means there will be some conversations that confront behaviors and issues that aren't comfortable. But we aren't called to be just great friends; we are called to be ambassadors for God, representing His interests. It takes humility, courage, and commitment on our part. The person we are leading may choose to be led no longer. They may reject us in the process. We have to care more about the person, their calling, and their relationship with God than their feelings about us. We have to be willing to risk the relationship in order to help them grow in their relationship with God.

Of course we must speak the truth in love. Discipleship and confrontation should never give us a feeling of satisfaction or joy. We have to say the right thing at the right time in the right way, but we must say it. If there is a conversation that can help them become more like Jesus or succeed in the areas of their lives, we should say it. If we refuse, we do them a disservice by attempting to preserve their feelings or our relationship. On the front end of the relationship, we may fail by speaking when we should be silent. Once we have gained influence, we may fail by being silent when we should speak.

We will give account to God for what He wanted us to say and we refused. God said in Ezekiel 3:18 that if He tells the prophet to warn a person and they do not, He will require the blood of the person at the hands of the prophet. To be a Second Mile Leader is to be a disciple maker. It is a holy and fearful task. We are to use our influence and leadership in their lives to make disciples. We are accountable, but we can do it. Jesus would have never asked us to do it if we could not.

Give Ourselves Away

Discipleship is about influence. We influence by serving. We serve best after we connect and know what the needs are. When we connect and serve, we can leverage influence to make disciples.

It's not mysterious or magical. If we will invest ourselves in the lives of others, we will gain the right and opportunity to help direct people's lives in the course that God planned for them long ago. We can help them to learn to obey all that Jesus commanded, and then they will become Second Mile Leader, too! They will be disciples who make disciples.

12

A SHEPHERD'S HEART

When he saw the crowds, he had compassion on them because they were confused and helpless, like sheep without a shepherd. (Matthew 9:36 NLT)

All my life I've had an issue with food. I like it. A lot. As a result, my body has never really been in shape, unless you consider round a shape. As a kid I was made fun of all the time. They used to make a pants size called "husky." Those were the ones I wore. It was a nice way of saying, "fat." My pants were politically correct before there was such a thing.

Several times I tried to conquer the blubber demon. I could not do it. When I asked the Lord for help, I discovered this kind comes out only by prayer, and fasting, and exercise. When I finally came to terms with the fact that fat doesn't just magically disappear, I knew for sure I had to go to the gym.

The problem is I don't like going to the gym. Not one bit. There's not one thing about working out I consider fun. You know those people who enjoy going to the gym every day? Some people call them gym rats. I call them psycho. There has to be something wrong for them to enjoy working out so much.

In several seasons of my life my dread for the gym became less than my disgust for my physical condition. I found my reason and motivation for going. For a season I went through a period of faithful workouts and diets. It really improved my health and physique.

Even though I had developed a habit of doing what I needed to do, I continued to need motivation. I had to find some inspiration, some mental trick, to compel myself to go to the gym every day. It never failed; when I woke up and it was time to work out, I was full of dread, not desire. I would tell myself, "You'll be proud of yourself when it's over," or "You'll feel better when you're done," or "Do it for your grandkids so you're able to play with them." I would go through all sorts of mental calisthenics before I ever did the physical ones. My natural desire was to sit on the couch with a bag of Kettle Cooked BBQ chips, not sweat on the Stairmaster. What I *wanted* and and what I *needed* were two different things.

My most successful season of faithful exercise came after reading a book by a fitness coach who challenged me to write down my reasons for getting healthy. I wrote down about five different reasons. Every morning I would recite those reasons to motivate myself to be faithful. Then I would get in the car and go to the gym. I had found my "why."

Find Your Why

As Second Mile Leaders, God is calling us into a ministry that will require us to be motivated by a "why." We will need a compelling reason to move out of what is natural and comfortable. We will need motivation to moves us from normal to necessary.

Our natural tendency is to be selfish, to withdraw. I would be lying if I told you that I always want to do what is in the best interest of others. More often than not, I want to do what is in the best interest of Jon. I would rather plop down in my easy chair in the air conditioning, turn up the volume on the surround sound system, shut out the world. Ironically I would likely choose to watch a story about someone doing the opposite of what I am doing in that moment. I would rather watch a movie about a hero than become one.

When I think of the people around me and the very real and heavy burdens they are carrying, it is overwhelming. I don't really know if I want to get involved. My life is already difficult. I convince myself to sit back and hold tight. I tell myself that if I wait a bit longer, someone else will most likely help them.

But God has called us to action. He has called us to pick up the wounded around us, throw them over our shoulders, and carry them to freedom. It's not easy, and it's often not fun.

To do what God is calling us to do requires moving beyond self interest, self-promotion, and self-preservation. We must adopt a mode of operation that is so counterintuitive it requires fuel by something bigger than our personal desires. We need a "why"–motivation that propels us forward.

Normal nominal Christians become great when they are filled with compassion.

A Motivating Force

This motivation comes from one word: Compassion. It fuels our efforts. It compels us into action. Compassion strips us from self-interested security and into others-oriented risk. Compassion causes us to do great things for God. It is the intangible component that makes us spring into action without a second thought. It gets us into the miracle zone–where we are way over our heads and in need of God. We come out heroes on the other side of the action, though being a hero never entered our minds. We just simply saw a soul in need. Normal nominal Christians become great when they are filled with compassion.

The Greek word for compassion used in the New Testament is *splagchnizomai*. One of its meanings is to be "moved in the bowels." The bowels were thought to be the seat of love and pity. If you've seen or heard something that made you have a deep pain in the pit of your stomach, you've probably had the feeling of compassion.

At times when I have been praying for people, compassion has overtaken me. At other times, something I saw or heard caused something to stir in the pit of my stomach. It felt as though someone had reached into my stomach, grabbed my intestines, and was twisting them together.

Compassion, however, isn't just the feeling of pity. It is an emotion that leads to action. Once compassion hits us, we can no longer be content to sit back and let someone else take care of the situation. We are moved into action.

The Bible speaks of Jesus being moved this way many times.

He is our model of what it looks like to be moved with a force that demands action. As we look at His life, put yourself in His shoes. Think of your life. Do some self-reflection. Ask yourself how you would respond if you were in the same situations as Christ. Would you make the same decisions?

If you are ready to become a Second Mile Leader, it is time to receive an impartation of compassion. Before we proceed, we need to confront complacency in our hearts and replace it with compassion. With hearts filled with compassion, Jesus can use us in His effort to redeem and restore the world.

Jesus, Our Example

The setting begins with Jesus' cousin, John the Baptist, in prison. He has been there for some time. At one point, he sent word to Jesus asking if He was indeed the Messiah. I believe part of this question John asked had to do with his own future. John was wondering if Jesus was going to rise to power, establish His throne, and free him from prison. While Jesus could have intervened in John's situation and exercised his power to set him free, doing so did not align with His purpose on the Earth. John remained in jail, and so Jesus gets some bad news a bit later about His beloved cousin.

> So John was beheaded in the prison, and his head was brought on a tray and given to the girl, who took it to her mother. Later, John's disciples came for his body and buried it. Then they went and told Jesus what had happened. As soon as Jesus heard the news, he left in a boat

to a remote area to be alone. (Matthew 14:10-13 NLT)

How Jesus responds is very human. It is exactly what I would want to do in this situation. I would want to withdraw from everyone and have my time of private sorrow. John has just been murdered. Jesus wants some time to go away and deal with the emotion of the moment. He needs some time to Himself. He needs to cry and mourn. This seems more than fair. Jesus, the God-man who is always working miracles on behalf of others, needs some "me time."

He headed for a place where he could be by Himself. He had plans to go away and deal with the pain. The only problem was that people figured out where He was going. They still wanted something from Him. They knew Jesus had answers to their pain and problems. They needed Him. In their minds, it couldn't wait. So they headed where He was going and arrived there first.

> *But the crowds heard where he was headed and followed on foot from many towns. Jesus saw the huge crowd as he stepped from the boat, and **he had compassion on them** and healed their sick. That evening the disciples came to him and said, "This is a remote place, and it's already getting late. Send the crowds away so they can go to the villages and buy food for themselves." But Jesus said, "That isn't necessary - you feed them." (Matthew 14:13b-16 NLT)*

Jesus healed their sick even though His cousin had just been murdered. Why? He saw the crowd, and "He had compassion on them." Compassion changed his intentions. His attention was diverted from His own needs to the needs of others. It moved Him to action. No longer focused on His own pain, Jesus saw theirs instead. He healed them.

Compassion makes you feel for others when you may already be hurting yourself.

The disciples had a different attitude and desire. As evening approached, they felt that they had discharged their duty. It was time to pull up a chair and sit for a while. They asked Jesus to send the crowd away. They wanted their work to be done. Jesus' response shocked them. He essentially said, "I'm extending the workday. Find some food. I want you to feed them." Not only were they surprised with the request for extra effort and time, they were overwhelmed at the need. They didn't have enough resources to do what Jesus was commanding.

This scene demonstrates exactly what Jesus will continue to ask of us. He modeled what it means to be a Second Mile Leader. While it was within His right to go and mourn His situation, He chose to set aside His needs and desires to serve others. Then in turn, He challenged his disciples to do the same.

As we choose to become Second Mile Leaders and begin to connect with those around us, we will be presented with hundreds of opportunities to live and love like Jesus. When faced with those moments, what will we choose–serve the people or send them away?

Jesus had compassion. He felt something deeply for these people. His physical response to the condition of those around Him motivated Him to serve when He didn't feel like it. Compassion makes you feel for others when you may already be hurting yourself.

The disciples wanted the multitudes to fend for themselves. Jesus said, "No, you feed them." This is what Jesus wants to do with you and me. He wants to feed people through our efforts and our compassion.

Yet we usually prefer to send people away. We will not want to care for them. We are normally self-centered, not others-oriented. Why? We aren't moved with compassion. To be a Second Mile Leader, we must be characterized by self-sacrifice motivated by compassion.

Motivated By Spiritual Sight

We need to be able to draw the contrast between the current condition and the desired destination. We need a clear and compelling vision to move people from where they are to where they need to be. This insight provides a framework for understanding where people are and, therefore, for what must be done.

Once we have a picture of what we are to do, compassion moves us to action. It's not enough just to know where people are and where they need to go. Leaders step into the situation and do something about it. Compassion becomes the fuel that propels us forward. We become motivated by spiritual sight. This spiritual sight is what moved Jesus into action.

*Jesus traveled through all the towns and villages of that area, teaching in the synagogues and announcing the Good News about the Kingdom. And he healed every kind of disease and illness. When **he saw** the crowds, **he had compassion on them because they were confused and helpless, like sheep without a shepherd.** (Matthew 9:35-36 NLT)*

Note the progression. First, Jesus saw them. He was looking outward. Many of us do not see the need because we are not looking. Sometimes we just want to close our eyes to the realities in the world and ignore the need around us. Jesus did not do this. He saw because he was looking. Are you looking?

Second, when Jesus saw them, He didn't see their skin. He saw their situation. They were confused and helpless. The outcome of confusion and helplessness was every sort of death. If Jesus had taken note that these people were clear minded and certain of direction, He could simply have kept walking. He knew, however, that these people were in a state that without intervention would lead to their demise.

With this revelation, compassion filled Jesus. He was motivated as a leader. He knew it was His responsibility to do something about the condition of these people He had encountered. He saw the contrast between where people were and where they should be. They were sheep without a shepherd. They needed one. He chose to be one.

Sheep need shepherds to keep them from becoming the victims of their own choices. Sheep eat the grass around them until the ground is bare dirt. They pollute the soil on which they graze until it breeds parasites that will infect and kill them. They will drink polluted water. Their instinct to follow the herd is so strong that entire herds of sheep have been known to walk off a cliff because one of them fell from it.

Without leaders to shepherd and guide their lives, people act just like sheep. They will become victims of their own appetites and ignorance. They will wallow in filth. They will do what seems best to them, not realizing all the while they are destroying themselves. Without shepherds sheep die.

Are we willing to be shepherds? Are we willing to get into their worlds, their mistakes, the filth of the sins in their lives? Will we be the ones who make a difference by our presence? Instead of condemning them, yelling at them, and ostracising them, will we become a shepherd in order to save them?

**Compassion will do whatever it takes
to touch and heal people.**

Propelled Into Action

Jesus never stopped at the emotion that compassion provokes. He allowed that emotion to propel Him into action. The question for us is "Will we shut down the feeling or allow that feeling to move us to make a difference?" Compassion that is shut down is no better than pity, but compassion unleashed becomes a powerful force to set people free.

Another gospel's account of Jesus seeking solitude following the news of John's death records another aspect of what compassion compelled Jesus to do.

> *So they left by boat for a quiet place, where they could be alone. But many people recognized them and saw them leaving, and people from many towns ran ahead along the shore and got there ahead of them. Jesus saw the huge crowd as he stepped from the boat, and **he had compassion on them** because they were like sheep without a shepherd. **So** he began teaching them many things. (Mark 6:32-34 NLT)*

The wording is powerful: He had compassion on them, **so**…! Jesus sprang into action. He didn't just shake his head and say, "That's bad, guys. Look at those poor people. What a shame!" No! He got busy doing something about the situation. Jesus modeled for us that compassion will do *whatever it takes* to touch and heal people.

Gut Check

If you're not making time in your agenda during the week to be inconvenienced by the pain of the situations of others, you're probably not filled with compassion. We will prioritize our lives and reorder our schedules when we are filled with compassion.

If you have an attitude toward people that excludes them

rather than embraces them, you're probably not full of compassion. Jesus touched the leper; *then* He healed him. He risked exposure to their disease. He didn't wait for the disease to disappear before He came near. The church has long been characterized by excluding the lepers of the day. We require them to be clean before they can come near rather than making them clean by contact with the life of Christ in us.

If you're serving only where *you* enjoy serving, then you're probably not moved by and with compassion. Yes, we are designed by God perfectly for a place in the body of Christ, yet we often use our gifting and calling as an excuse *not* to serve. We say, "That's not my gifting," or "It's not my passion." We make it sound spiritual, but it's actually selfish. Just because we're not gifted or trained to be a doctor doesn't mean we can walk by a bleeding person and allow him to die just because we aren't "good at that."

If there's a task that's beneath you, you're not moved by compassion. I am blessed to have people that clean our building. If it's not clean, however, I don't have an excuse to walk by things that need to be addressed just because "I have people for that." Second Mile Leaders do not allow this attitude in their hearts.

If you can't catch the vision for what your church is doing to reach the lost in your community, you're probably not moved by compassion. Compassion comes when we see the spiritual condition and have the heart of God. So either we aren't looking or we are refusing the call of compassion, the heart of our Savior.

**Compassion frequently comes with a price—
the cost of comfort and convenience.**

Fuel For The Shepherd's Heart

A number of years ago our family was able to take a vacation at Disney World. We had been looking forward to this trip for years. Our children were excited. We were excited. We couldn't wait to see the Magic Kingdom and watch our children's expressions as they saw characters come to life that they had seen only in cartoons.

Aimee's parents joined us on the trip. It was a great time for them to spend with the grandkids. Plus they paid for half of the accommodations. We had built in babysitters and bank rollers—a win/win.

The trip was planned down to the minute. Aimee is a person who loves to research everything about a trip before we take it. She had read a book that specifically outlined the exact order we should ride the rides at Disney. She told us that if we trusted her and followed her crazy plan, we would be able to ride all the rides we wanted. We would also be free to go back to the room to swim and sleep, return later to ride more rides, and watch the fireworks at the closing of the park.

We did what she told us, and it went just as she said it would. We zigzagged all over the park, following what seemed to be a nonsensical plan. Our kids were having the time of their lives. It was amazing to see their faces light up every time a character from a Disney film appeared on the street. We stopped to get autographs and pictures. We laughed on the rides. And we were able to do all that we wanted to do. Other families without a plan might have ridden only three or four rides during the entire day, but thanks to Aimee's plan, we were exhausted but happy at the end of the day.

The whole trip was planned out like this. We had several days at the different Disney parks. Toward the end of the trip, we had planned a day at the beach. We knew we would need a day to relax and recuperate from all the hurried walking of the other days, so the last day would be a lazy one at the beach. Among the other firsts of the trip, the beach day was going to be the first time our kids had ever seen the ocean. We couldn't wait to relax and just enjoy the last day of our trip. It never happened.

In the middle of the last day at Disney, my father-in-law received a phone call with terrible news. His cousin and his cousin's son had been killed in a motor vehicle accident in southwestern Arkansas. The entire family was devastated. This cousin was very dear to Larry. He felt that we should immediately return to Arkansas to be with the family. We would stay with them and then attend the funeral.

Please don't judge me for what I am about to say. I was upset. I was upset that we were being asked to leave immediately. I did not know this cousin. I had never met him, and neither had my children. I felt like we should not have to cut the vacation short and return to Arkansas days before the funeral. I suggested we take Larry and Georgiann to the airport to catch a flight. Aimee and I would finish the vacation. We would join them two days later in Arkansas in time for the funeral. I thought our kids should not have to lose out on something they had been looking forward to. I wanted to put *our* family first.

This put Aimee in a very difficult position. On one hand, she had a husband and children who were not going to be able finish their vacation and see the ocean as promised. They didn't know her cousin. Was it really fair to cut their vacation short to have them go sit in an Atlanta, Texas, hotel room for two days while the family gathered and made arrangements? On the other hand, she *did* know this cousin. They had been great friends all of their years growing up. She knew it was important for her to go. It was the right and honorable thing to do.

We chose to return to Arkansas. To this day, I can still remember the tension in my heart as we drove through the night to get back to Arkansas. I felt guilty. What my kids wanted, even *deserved*, had been taken from them. Doing what was right felt so wrong. At the same time, I felt like a horrible person. How could I *not* embrace the idea that the trip home was the right one?

This is the tension a person with a shepherd's heart, a Second Mile Leader, will face. Do we do what we *want* or what others *need*? I'm not advocating that we sacrifice our families for ministry, but our families might need to sacrifice for ministry.

We might be faced with hard choices like these and be confronted with the reality that the mission is greater than me. Mourning may have to be paused. "Me time" might have to be postponed. Saying "no" might not be an option in the moment. Compassion compels us to act and change the world of the people around us. It frequently comes with a price—the cost of comfort and convenience.

When we really see the way Jesus sees–when we realize that the spiritual condition of people is more important than the temporal desires we have–we are beginning to be moved with compassion. When we really have the heart of our Savior, we won't be able to sit back and do nothing while people around us suffer like sheep without shepherds. We will be compelled to be difference makers. In order to be effective as Second Mile Leaders, we must have a heart that is filled with compassion.

What will change your agenda? What will cause you to open your home or answer your phone? What will cause you to get up and go help someone move, pray for them, visit them in the hospital? What will cause you to serve others when it's the least convenient thing for you? One thing–Compassion. It is the fuel that powers the heart of a shepherd.

Prayer For A Shepherd's Heart

At this point, you may be struck with a realization that you're not motivated by the needs of others. Maybe you have not yet seen any real spiritual problems in the lives of people around you. Of course you see issues in the lives of people around you, but you don't really see anything spiritual about it. To you it has always seemed superficial. You think that a simple set of behaviors being changed will make things just fine. You need the sight of our Savior. You need fresh eyes.

Perhaps you do have spiritual eyes. You have seen the people around you from a perspective that recognizes their spiritual condition, but you realize you've done little with that knowledge. Perhaps from time to time you have been moved to pray earnestly and fervently that Jesus would do something about their condition. You might have attempted to serve them and make a difference in their lives. Somewhere along the way though you realize now that you've shunted the Spirit's draw in your heart and diverted that desire until it no longer propels you into action. You see, but you don't do. You need fresh fire.

Maybe you've worked hard for a long time and you've just hit a wall. You have faithfully served in your church. You worked with people to rebuild their lives according to God's plan. Now you find yourself without any more energy. You really do love people; you're just tired. You need more fuel.

Whether you need fresh eyes, fresh fire, or more fuel, God wants to fill you with compassion. In the passage from Matthew we read earlier, Jesus was moved with compassion when He saw the spiritual condition of the people. Notice what He says next:

> *The harvest is great, but the workers are few. So pray to the Lord who is in charge of the harvest; ask him to send more workers into his fields." (Matthew 9:37-38 NLT)*

Jesus was being a bit sneaky here. He was telling His disciples to pray that God would send out more workers. The disciples may not have realized they were praying for themselves. The very next thing Jesus does in Matthew chapter 10 is to send His disciples out to minister and labor in the field. He wanted them to pray for the laborers so He could fill them with compassion and turn them into laborers. In Matthew 10:1-5 He called them, then gave them authority, then sent them. Jesus is still doing this today. He is calling, commissioning, and sending people as laborers, servants and shepherds into the fields to labor. This process begins with a prayer, "God, send laborers." This is actually the prayer: "God, send *me*."

If you're needing eyes to see, desire reignited, or fuel to continue in the harvest, I want to give you a prayer to pray over yourself. We need to pray that Jesus will impart His heart to us. We need to pray for Him to fill us with compassion. We need Him to help us see what He sees, love as He loves, and act as He acts. When this happens, we will finally be ready to be sent into the harvest because we have a shepherd's heart.

Pray this prayer with me:

Father, I ask you to send me into the harvest. Give me the heart of a shepherd as Jesus had. Help me see people as you see them—not by their outward appearance but their spiritual condition. Give me a vision of where these children of yours should be in contrast to where they are. Help me to be filled with compassion, not pity. Let that compassion push me into action. Help me not shut off the emotion or turn my attention away from the pain around me. Instead let me be compelled to act as Jesus would act if He were here. As I go, keep me filled with compassion. Help me run when I am weary because I'm filled with the driving force of your heartbeat. I ask you to impart to me the heart of a true disciple. Make me a person that is focused on others and not myself. Give me a desire to invest my life into those around me. Father, in this moment, I receive a shepherd's heart. In Jesus' name, Amen.

I believe that from this point forward you will begin to see differently, feel deeply, and serve freely as you love from

A SHEPHERD'S HEART.

13

RELATIONAL CURRENCY

Better to trust the man who is frequently in error

than the one who is never in doubt.

- Eric Sevareid

Growing up, our family went fishing a lot. We had two ponds on the property where we lived and plenty of worms we could dig up in the front yard. It was a normal to see my dad, my brother, or a friend strolling through the field on his way to try his luck that afternoon.

When I would go fishing, I never seemed to have any luck catching fish. I would catch branches of trees under the water. After spending some time trying to free the line, I would end up snapping it. I would spend the next several minutes trying to reset everything so I could try again.

Sometimes my bobber would suddenly get jerked under the water, signalling I was getting a bite. I would get so excited. Many times it was just a huge turtle on the end of the line, so I would cut my line and start all over again. If I did catch a fish, it was usually a sun perch–something not even worth keeping. Disappointed, I'd throw it back and try again.

This was my normal fishing experience. I honestly don't remember landing a fish that was large enough to keep and take home for dinner. My brother caught some. My dad caught some. Not me. I do remember hooking a couple of big ones, but my line broke before I got them to the shore. I quit fishing. I simply no longer trusted that if I went I would have a good experience.

The story parallels something that happens in relationships every day. People give up on them simply because their trust is gone. Because of past experiences, they no longer believe a conversation will go well. They don't believe the person will listen, care, or change. "It's just not worth trying," they think. So they just walk away.

Emotional Currency

Relationships run on an emotional currency. It is invisible but tangible. This currency keeps relationships sustained, alive, and connected. This relational currency is trust.

John Maxwell describes trust in a relationship like having change in your pocket. The more you build trust with someone, the more change you accumulate. If you have change in your pocket and something negative happens, the relationship will be able to continue. The change in your pocket covers the negative experience.

From a missed meeting to a broken promise, emotional currency of trust is used to sustain the relationship. As long as you haven't run out of trust, the relationship will remain intact.

If our withdrawals exceed our deposits, we bankrupt the relationship. At this point, the relationship breaks. We are out of trust.

It's over, and we don't realize it until it's too late. To sustain relationships, we have to continue making deposits of trust to strengthen the relationship.

Trust is defined as reliance on the integrity or strength of a person. It is confidence. People are willing to place their lives in someone's hands because they are confident they will take care of them and do what they want or need. They believe this person won't let them down. Trust is demonstrated through reliance.

**Relationships will grow deeper as a
track record of trustworthiness is created.**

Several years ago I had a couple of cloth folding chairs break when I sat on them. After the first one, I was a bit leery. After the second one, I was done with that type of chairs. I chose to sit on very uncomfortable bleachers instead of risking more injury in the more comfortable folding chairs. I just didn't trust them anymore. When they let me down (literally), I decided I'd be better off with a sore back from the bleacher than a bruised ego from the dirt.

People have the same reaction in relationships. After deciding someone in their life is no longer trustworthy, they abandon one relationship for another that they consider safer. As you begin to lead, keep this in mind. When people have been hurt over and over in relationships, they may have trouble trusting you. Their low trust may have nothing to do with you and everything to do with their history. They need assurance that if they put their trust in you it won't cause them more pain. It may take some time for them to gain the confidence that you're not like the last leader they followed or last friend they had.

Gaining the trust of those you lead requires answering certain unspoken, emotional questions people have in their minds. You have probably noticed that most relationships start off fairly shallow and deepen over time. Relationships will grow deeper as a track record of trustworthiness is created.

In order for people to serve in positions with top-secret security clearance for the United States, a candidate must undergo a stringent background check and pass several evaluations. With each successful test, the candidate reaches higher and higher levels of trust.

You may not realize it, but people do the same thing in relationships. Each relationship undergoes subtle tests before trust deepens. With each successful test, people grant higher levels of access to the deeper part of who they are. These questions are not typically verbalized. Instead they are presented as certain situational challenges. They are trust tests. If the examinee passes, more access is given. If he fails, he is locked out of levels to which he previously had access.

Since these are situational evaluations rather than verbal questions, I have included a few of them here. As you read them, reflect on whether you would pass the "yes" test of these assessments. If you cannot honestly answer yes to each of these, you will need to work on these issues. A proven track record is required before people will put their lives in your hands.

The Assessments

Assessment 1: Do You Care?

It's been said that people don't care how much you know until they know how much you care. This is so incredibly true. People are looking for someone to walk through life with. They need a friend they can count on when they hit a rough patch in life. They want a trusted companion–someone they know will answer the phone or drive across town to sit with them in their darkest hour.

Listen Up

In his book, *The Seven Habits of Highly Effective People*, Steven Covey says one habit that we should develop is to seek *first* to understand, *then* to be understood. Notice the order. Highly effective people seek to understand rather than demanding to be heard and understood. Covey says the deepest need of the human heart is to be understood. If we can lead in seeking first to understand, it demonstrates tremendous care on our parts. It shows that you're interested not just in them learning about you; you're interested in learning about them.

Listening well communicates that you would answer your phone if they needed you, that you will pray for them when they ask you to, that you will notice if they are missing from your circle and reach out to them, and that you would visit them if they were sick. The essence of this care is that you will make *their* needs a priority in *your* life.

I've met so many people who are ignorant of the amount of talking they do. They are sadly unaware that they monopolize conversations. In dominating the conversation, they communicate a subtle truth, "I care more about me than about you."

If your conversations are typified by you doing the majority of talking or trying to make your point, you're likely not deepening trust with people around you. You may have many friends, but the amount of deep sharing that happens in your conversations is probably low. It takes trust for that level of sharing to happen.

Unless you have a specific request or reason to be the primary speaker in a given setting, you listen much more than you speak. The next time you're with your friends, pay attention to how long you're talking. If you're dominating the conversation, flip the script.

When you listen to a person–really listen to them–you build a sense of trust because you are demonstrating that you care about *them*. This care shows that you value them as a person, not just a means to an end.

**When someone opens his heart to you,
it is an ultimate test of your *CARE*acter.**

Sacred Moments

We've all had a conversation with friends or children in which they shared something that shifted the entire feel of the conversation. They made themselves vulnerable. They might have shared a fear, a failure, a grief, a shame, or a secret they've held onto for years. In that moment, they trusted you with something they seldom share with others. You were allowed into an inner chamber of their heart. The conversation to this point might have been casual or serious, but now it has become sacred.

How we respond to this moment of vulnerability will determine if we are let in or locked out of their hearts in the future. If we take this moment for granted, it communicates a lack of care and concern. Worse, if we scorn or ridicule them for what they share, we will permanently be locked out of their lives. Make no mistake, when people open their heart to you, this is an ultimate test of your **CARE**acter.

In a parenting class we took years ago called "Growing Kids God's Way," Gary Ezzo taught us this profound truth. It has stuck with me all these years. He taught us to be careful with your children's hearts when they open the door in a moment of vulnerability. How you respond will teach them about your care for them. If you don't demonstrate compassion, love, and concern, they will learn that you can't be trusted with their heart. Then they won't bother to share it with you any more.

I know many parents that feel they've been locked out of their children's hearts. I give them this same lesson. Keep pressing into the conversation until you recapture their hearts. Show them you can be trusted because you listen with empathy, you don't overreact when they share their failures, and you always demonstrate compassion and love even if correction is necessary.

To this day, I do my best to pay attention when the conversations with my children shift from small talk to heart talk. When it does, I do my best to put all distractions aside and stick with the conversation until *they* are finished talking.

This is not just important for conversations with my children. It's important for those I lead, as well. When they begin to share, I put aside distractions. I don't engage in other conversations, answer my phone, or return electronic communications.

If you and I can listen more than we speak and lean in during those sacred moments, we will demonstrate that we really have a genuine care. Change will be deposited into our trust account, and the relationship will deepen.

A true leader does not leverage others for himself.
He leverages himself for the benefit of others.

Assessment 2: Are You Loyal?

Loyalty is a big deal in relationships. People want to know that you're going to remain in their corner, not defect to the other side when it seems more beneficial to you. They don't want to be friends with someone who's wishy-washy, looking for relationships that last until they can no longer be leveraged for the next rung on the ladder of success.

We demonstrate loyalty to people by using our lives to benefit them. If you're using people for what they do for you, you've got it backwards. A true leader does not leverage others for himself. He leverages himself for the benefit of others. Our lives should be consumed on behalf of the people around us. Are you taking from people or are you giving yourself away to them? Trust will deepen as they see you're in it for them and not for yourself. Remain loyal to people. Don't use them to your advantage or walk over them when you get a better opportunity.

When I was a kid, we did crazy things like shoot fireworks at each other. One night when we were doing this, I pretended to defect to our opponent only to throw lit fireworks at his feet. I thought it was absolutely hilarious. He didn't. It just so happened that he already had a bottle rocket lit in a tube while he was dancing to avoid the firecrackers I threw at his feet. My plan backfired when his lit bottle rocket launched and flew into my side of the battle, landing in my stash of fireworks and setting them off. I lost a lot of my fireworks, and he got his revenge.

This same thing plays out in our relationships when we defect from one side to the other. If you are having tension in your relationship with someone, don't move across the aisle to form alliances with someone else. This is a huge disloyalty and one from which the relationship may never recover. Disagreement is not a reason to become disloyal. Instead we should work to resolve the conflict and come to a better solution. Don't play the political game, moving back and forth between convenient relationships in order to get your way. This will bankrupt your trust and break your relationships.

Assessment 3: Will You Keep My Confidence?

There are a couple people in my life I never tell about a surprise I have planned for someone. From a gift I purchased to a surprise birthday party, they simply can't keep it secret. They're not being malicious; they're just excited and forget it's supposed to be surprise. Regardless of their motives, it makes me very angry when they let the cat out of the bag.

Did you ever hear the phrase "Loose lips sink ships"? That is these people. The surest way for everyone to find out what you want no one to know is to tell them. If you're that person, you'll never be a trusted leader.

For people to share their hearts and lives with you, they have to know that you will keep their confidence. They need to know you are not the type of person who lets secrets slip on accident or, worse yet, the person who loves to share the latest juicy gossip he's learned.

We've all seen the movies with a "leak" in some administration or government. When they find the source of the leak, it is plugged. The person is terminated or cut off from future information.

When people trust us with the deep things in our lives, they should be treated as top secret. We should never share the information with anyone, even someone we are certain is trustworthy. The problem with thinking we can just share with the "one person" is that one person also has "one person" he feels he can trust as well. Before you know it, a chain of highly trusted individuals will have been given top secret information with which you alone were entrusted. If you're discovered to be the leak of someone's secret information, he will cut you off from it in the future. Whatever leadership you had will be gone.

Keeping confidence means we cover rather than expose. The Bible tells us love covers a multitude of sin. This doesn't mean love *ignores* sin; it just doesn't go and shout it from the rooftop. Love confronts sin privately. Jesus laid out clear procedures for how to confront a brother, giving him the opportunity to repent privately. Only after our private attempts at correction have been ignored do we bring others into the conversation.

Typically when people share a sin or area of struggle in their lives, they are doing it so you can help them to repent and recover from its effects. Our job is to forgive them, pray for them, and hold them accountable. If we do this, we help them overcome the trap of the sin that has held them captive.

If we tell others about what they've done, we demonstrate extreme disloyalty. People will no longer trust us with things they need help with. They will fear you just want to get "dirt" you can use against them.

Never expose a person's secrets or sins to others. Whether it's a slip of the tongue or a moment of jest where we reveal something about them to someone else, the effects are the same. The hurt is deep, and often the trust cannot be rebuilt.

An exception to this might be when you need help to resolve the situation. It is fine to ask your leader or pastor over this person for wisdom and assistance. In this case, you're asking a spiritual authority above you how to deal with the situation. Yet even in this circumstance, we should attempt to ask for help in a way that keeps the person's identity secret (unless the person is about to harm himself or someone else or has refused correction).

I like to think of keeping confidence of people in terms of the laws surrounding medical recordkeeping. The Health Insurance Portability and Accountability Act of 1996 (HIPAA) provides guidelines for sharing information regarding patient medical information. One of the provisions of HIPAA is that you can share information with other health care providers regarding a patient only to the level that it is pertinent to their care. If the other health care provider doesn't need to know, you don't tell them. Anything more is considered a violation of privacy.

This is how we should treat information divulged in relationship with those around us. Keep confidences, and trust will increase. If we are people who reveal or expose, we may find we have a position of authority but no real influence.

Assessment 4: Will You Follow Through?

We all know people who promise they will attend an event, show up to help, or return something they have borrowed, but they never do. Sadly we are never surprised when they fail to follow through. You probably have that person in mind right now, don't you?

These unfaithful and unreliable people can't really be trusted. They may be likeable in all aspects of their personality, but they simply never follow through on their promises.

There was a time in our country when a man's word was his bond. There was no need for litigation in court. People of integrity simply did what they said they were going to do. If keeping your word was inconvenient or painful, it didn't matter. People lived by Psalm 15:4, where righteous men "keep their promises even when it hurts." In days gone by, people would be slow to promise because they knew they needed to be quick to deliver.

Today it's the opposite. We are quick to promise and slow to deliver. Integrity is low. Compromise is high. People are full of excuses instead of resolve.

To be effective leaders, we cannot be people who fail to follow through. We have to do what we say we are going to do. If we make plans for dinner, schedule an appointment, promise to pray for someone, or commit to call, we must do what we said we would.

I have failed to show up for appointments before and have seen and felt the disappointment. Having learned my lesson, I do my best to follow through. I use the calendar in my phone with tremendous discipline. I have many things competing for my attention, and because I'm often distracted I make sure I make note of appointments I am supposed to be keeping. If you ever catch me on the tail of a conversation where I've made a commitment, you may struggle to gain my attention while I finish scheduling an appointment in my calendar. I know just how important it is to follow through with the person I just made a commitment to. I also know that if I fail to put it in my calendar immediately, I will probably forget to do what I just said I would do. Innocent or not, it will communicate that I don't value them and I can't be trusted. I cannot afford the inattention to my intentions.

When we keep our commitments, even if it hurts us, people notice, and their trust in us goes up. We have to follow through to continue to build trust.

Assessment 5: Can Your Leader Trust You?

Your pastor is ultimately responsible for the people and the area of ministry for which you are about to begin leading. Many leaders struggle to delegate authority and responsibility because the leaders they have had in the past have proven unreliable. Whether they treated people poorly or failed to follow through, they were burned in the process.

People may have been hurt in a moment when a department or ministry leader lashed out in anger or neglected his responsibility. Emotionally wounded, these people might have walked away from the church, not because of interaction with the main leader but because of a leader who was trusted with delegated authority.

Your pastor *wants* to trust you. He wants to empower you. He wants to "give you the keys," so to speak, but you have to be a person who is worthy of the trust you are about to be given. The areas we have covered so far will go a long way in assuring your delegated authority will be carried out with honor and trustworthiness. Below I've included a few more.

Fleecing The Flock

Never leverage your relationships in an organization for personal gain. As you become a leader, you will likely be given a list of names and phone numbers. You will be given a position from which you can leverage influence. Take care that you do not leverage this position for what can benefit you. If you do such things as trying to get people onboard with a multilevel marketing company, promoting your personal businesses, or attempting to borrow money, you have abused trust. These actions undermine your leadership ability. Furthermore, since the leaders above you entrusted you with this position, your actions cast a shadow of doubt on them. Since those you lead know the leaders supposedly vetted you before they entrusted you, their judgment is called into question. Your personal breach of trust causes organization-wide breach of trust.

Upward Loyalty

Many times when you are in a role closer to the people, they will bring their complaints about the direction, vision, or methodology of the organization to you. They will try to form an alliance with you against upper level leaders or pastors. Hoping you will become their liaison, they endear themselves to you, attempting to leverage your position for change in the organization.

Your leader wants to know if he can trust you not to become disloyal in the role you've been given. Your role is not to represent the people to your leader, but your leader to the people.

When people come to you and voice their complaints, you must take care that your heart does not begin to shift away from loyalty to the leader and toward a divisive spirit in your heart. Allowing disloyalty to slip in exposes you to the same spirit that motivated Absalom–one that says, "If I were king, I would...."

The rebellion in Absalom's heart caused a divide in the Kingdom. He stood in a place between the king and the people and lobbied for power. He stole the hearts of the people and divided the kingdom.

Just as this action divided Israel, it will do the same to your church. The people we are leading become collateral damage in the selfish struggle for power. This is not God's plan or will.

Remember that if you follow your leader and he is wrong, he takes the hit on credibility. He is accountable to God. When you go a different direction from your leader, however, you're wrong, even if you're right.

So how do we deal with our grievances and issues? The following are some tips.

Dealing With Grievances

When you have issues with your leader's decisions, do not share it with a peer or someone you lead; instead, bring it directly to your leader and have the conversation in private. Ask questions for clarification. Seek to understand why the decision is made. Chances are that if you have the information the leader has you will see that the decision is a pretty good one.

If the leader has information that he cannot strategically or ethically divulge, however, you might leave with the same questions with which you came. In this moment, you simply have to trust him by knowing his character and his track record. What do you know about your leader? Is he characterized by making decisions that are in the right interest of the people? Give him the benefit of the doubt. He likely does that for you on a regular basis.

From time to time, you will disagree with his decision even after meeting and discussing the situation. If you were in his chair, you would do things differently, but you are not in his chair. So how you behave from this point is critical.

You have challenged decisions privately; now, you champion them publicly. This can be difficult, but it is important. Never allow your disagreement with your leader to become public. If you do, it won't be long until you have a following that is loyal to you but not to your leader. To shut this down, publicly praise your leader's wisdom and decisions. To do otherwise is to cause confusion and division, maybe even leading some to stray from the church.

Jesus had strong words for anyone who would cause a young

one to stumble in the faith. He said it would be better for us to *"have a large millstone tied around your neck and be drowned in the depths of the sea" (Matthew 18:6 NLT).* Those are strong words we should remember. Jesus is never pleased when we cause confusion and division. As a result, many people end up hurt and out of the faith in the process of our grab for power. It's never the right way.

Candid Honor

Good leaders like to know what you're thinking. You might think you would rather not bother them or might even be afraid of their reaction. Chances are, though, they would welcome the conversation and the challenge. You might be bringing a perspective to the table they have not considered.

When your leader sees you consistently challenging in private but championing in public, he will know that your intention is to cover him, not expose him. He will trust you and thank you for your candor in private meetings.

When a decision is made that we don't understand, most of the time we should assume it was made for our benefit and move on. We are an entitled bunch because we live in the United States, and we feel we should have the right to question everything.

Decisions are made at times, however, that cause us to question the wisdom of, or worse yet, the character of our leaders. In this situation, our best move is to have a conversation so we can clear the air and keep our hearts pure.

The more we keep questions to ourselves, the more we find ways to give them wrong answers. We begin to question motives, not decisions. Disloyalty begins to rise in our hearts. We lose our trust in our leaders when a simple, five-minute conversation would clear the air and erase doubts.

While we might think that avoiding conflict is protecting us from uncomfortable conversations, it's actually allowing a wedge of distrust to form in our hearts. Avoiding the conversation leads to avoiding the person. The distance in our hearts becomes a physical distance. Have the conversation to cut out the doubt before it festers.

Receiving Feedback

We have blind spots. It's hard to see our own deficiencies. We all need another perspective regarding our decisionmaking and the execution of our leadership roles. This is where feedback, coaching, and correction come in.

If you cannot receive constructive criticism, correction, and coaching, you will never grow as a leader. If you are a thin-skinned person who is unable to receive correction, chances are you might have already been passed over for leadership. The leaders in your area might be afraid to empower you with authority. They know that when they need to give you feedback you won't receive it well. Rather than hurt your feelings and deal with the consequences, they might choose someone else they can coach more easily.

Since coaching and correction produce growth, we should actually desire and seek it out. If you're not a person who frequently asks for genuine feedback on whatever work you produce, start asking for input and start growing.

Relational Currency

If we have trust, we will have plenty of emotional currency in our pockets to be entrusted with authority. We can then leverage that authority for the purpose of moving people closer to Jesus. Let's be people who can be trusted so we can move God's people forward in their purpose.

14

LEADING WITH AN OPEN HEART

By this everyone will know that you are
my disciples, if you love one another.
- (John 13:35 NIV)

I'm 6' 5" and 250 pounds–a pretty big guy. Unfortunately a small portion of it frequently collides with door frames, ceiling fans, and corners. A friend of mine once explained my problem. He said that big people like me occupy 110 percent of the space they *think* about. That extra 10 percent of my body that I don't consider causes me a lot of pain. I've hit my head, cracked open my chin, and cut open my lip. I've banged my head so many times I'm lucky to have a scalp at all. Just the day before I wrote this chapter, as I was hunched down under a low clearance area, I swung my head around only to slam it against a low hanging piece of metal. I promise I didn't swear. Out loud. The week before that I banged my elbow on the door of my bedroom as I was entering it. About 4 years ago while deer hunting, I slipped and fell, striking my elbow on a large boulder. Now every time I position my elbow just so on the tabletop, a tiny bone fragment on my elbow reminds me of that boulder. 110 percent of the space I think about is 10 percent too much!

An interesting thing happens when I get injured. I immediately grab the area of pain. Although my hand does nothing to soothe the pain, my body reacts to the injury without me giving it a second thought. I believe this action is my body's instinctive reaction to protect itself from additional injury. My subconscious neurological system reasons that if my hand covers the area, it will be protected, guarded from anything else happening.

When people cause us emotional pain, we react as well. We withdraw from relationships, guarding our hearts. We might pull away from a single person or all relationships in general. We protect ourselves from additional relational injury.

**Leadership in the church is impossible
for someone who won't open his heart.**

Don't Play It Safe

Closing ourselves off emotionally from people makes it very difficult to do ministry. Everything about ministry is relationship. Whether we are helping people grow in their relationship to God or become close to one another, it's all about relationship. The church has no other product to offer. We deal exclusively in essential and eternal relationships. Ministry and leadership in the church are impossible for someone who won't open his heart.

We need to come to terms with this reality: In order to lead effectively, we must open our hearts. This means we will always be exposed to potential emotional injury. In fact, it's likely to happen. Those we love the most, those we are closest to, have the ability to hurt us the most.

Yet the call of Jesus isn't to play it safe; it's to be right in the middle of relationships, exposed to potential pain. He never shied away from a challenge. He didn't shrink back from the possibility that He might be misunderstood or betrayed. Those closest to Him failed him, betrayed Him, and denied Him. They fled while He was being tried for false accusations. One of His very own disciples gave him up for 30 pieces of silver, leading to His arrest and crucifixion. Jesus wasn't a wimp. He was a strong leader who was able to live with a heart wide open, face the challenges, and forgive when they came as a result.

Jesus calls us into that same adventure, that same risk. He asks us to be willing to face rejection, forgive when it's the last thing we want to do, and engage the wounded. He calls us to the souls damaged by this world–those who will lash out at others in a moment's notice. He demands we exit our bubbles of safety and attack Hell head on.

**Jesus didn't call us to protect our hearts
and secure ourselves in safe zones.**

Jesus did all He asks us to do. He lived a life characterized by risk. He bucked the religious systems of the day. Instead of hanging around with those who were already safe inside, He went after the broken, the outcasts, and the rejects. Today we in the church love to shout at the world, telling them to be different. Jesus got close enough to show them how. We love to huddle safely in our sanctuaries; He had church in the sinner's house.

The religious leaders of the day challenged His approach. When they asked His disciples why He would dare hang out with the scum of society, Jesus made His reasoning very clear: *"Healthy people don't need a doctor—sick people do. I have come to call not those who think they are righteous, but those who know they are sinners"* *(Mark 2:17 NLT).*

Jesus didn't follow religious norms. He rejected anything that would keep Him from the people He was here to reach. He got close to "sick" people. He was a friend of sinners. He didn't wait for them to come to the sanctuary to find salvation. He brought it to the dinner table.

Being around sick people carries with it the risk of becoming infected ourselves. Maybe that's why we like to huddle safely in services with saints rather than hang with the sinners in the streets. It's just less risky. Besides, if they really want Jesus they know where to find Him, right? We'll be right here when they decide to get right with God.

But Jesus didn't call us to protect our hearts and secure ourselves in safe zones. He called us to emulate Him. Be a doctor. Go where the sick people are. Take the medicine of the good news where people need it most.

Personal Protective Equipment

I loved working on the ambulance, helping people when they needed it most. Human behavior is interesting. When an accident happens, a crowd tends to gather. People love to have a front row seat when crazy things happen. They may even pull out their phones and start live streaming to social media. They don't want to help; they just want to see.

While everyone else is free to stand around and watch, EMTs have a duty to help those who are hurting. They don't have an option. Their duty to act means they have to do their best to aid the ailing, heal the hurting. They do this risking exposure and injury themselves. That's why part of the training to become an EMT includes how to protect yourself from exposure to the very diseases you're treating. There are precautions you take on every call, and there are precautions you take on *certain* calls. Depending on the nature of the illness or injury, you might need to wear specific personal protective equipment so you don't catch the disease you're trying to cure.

Leaders in the church risk exposure to the sicknesses of sin. Just as protections exist in the medical field, they exist in ministry as well. If we don't take certain precautions while helping others, we can become infected with the same sin-sickness they are carrying. Putting these protections in place will help keep us from being infected and to continue leading with an open heart. I've listed a few we need for basic protection below.

Forgiveness

Jesus tells a story in Matthew 18 of a person who owed a

large debt and was forgiven it. The forgiven man immediately went out and found a fellow servant who owed him a very small debt. Instead of extending the same grace of forgiveness he had just been shown, he had him thrown into prison until he could pay. When the master discovered his servant had acted so callously, he is incensed.

> *"Then the master called the servant in. 'You wicked servant,' he said, 'I canceled all that debt of yours because you begged me to. Shouldn't you have had mercy on your fellow servant just as I had on you?' In anger his master turned him over to the jailers to be tortured, until he should pay back all he owed. "This is how my heavenly Father will treat each of you unless you forgive your brother from your heart." (Matthew 18:21:32-35 NIV)*

Jesus finished the story with a comparison to our Father's expectation of us. *Forgive.* When people offend you, keep the right perspective. Don't think of the forgiveness they need from you; think of the forgiveness you received from God.

When we live life with a view of what we have been forgiven, it is much easier to forgive other people.

In this story one man owed more than he could ever repay in a lifetime. Upon his forgiveness, he demanded a negligible debt be repaid; when he was forgiven it, he demanded a minimal debt be paid immediately. It didn't take him long to forget just how much he had been forgiven. Jesus compares the master to God–forgiving the unforgivable, uncollectable debt. The parable paints the picture of our sin against God in contrast to man's sin against us. With His own blood, He forgave what we owed Him–a debt we could never pay.

In contrast He compares the worst infringements we face from others to a small, inconsequential debt. While we may think the offenses are large and unforgivable, Jesus is telling us that *in comparison* they are small. When we live life with a view of what we have been forgiven, it is much easier to forgive other people. The gratitude in our hearts gives us grace to forgive others.

We seem to forget this large discrepancy. The debt seems too big to forgive. The pain of what they did to us consumes us. We refuse to let them go. We demand they pay back all they owe us. Yet Jesus makes it clear that forgiveness is not optional. It doesn't matter if it's easy; it's expected.

In ministry people will do things that require you to forgive. Despite the fact that you are doing the best you can, the best you know how, they will be offended, claiming that you've failed them somehow. They might walk away from your team, small group, or church after you've poured countless hours into their lives. They might slander or malign you to others.

While we will have many opportunities to be offended with those we lead, we have to be able to "let it go." We must choose to walk in forgiveness. If we do not, our hearts will close to people. Bitterness will creep in and corrupt us. Compassion for people will be shut off. We will become callous and indifferent to the plight of those around us. The grace of God will evaporate from our lives. We will feel disconnected from God, people, and our calling.

Unforgiveness might feel good. It might bring you some sense of comfort and validation to keep records of wrongs or hold grudges. Yet unforgiveness carries with it a significant deception. We feel we are punishing the person who has wronged us by keeping them at a distance, demanding they pay us back for what they did. But the only person we are hurting is ourselves. It's been said that holding on to resentment is like drinking poison and expecting the other person to die.

Quite often the person we refuse to forgive is unaware he has hurt us. Even if he knew or remembered what he did, there's frequently nothing he can actually do to right the wrong. The only restitution he can make is an apology. The better choice is to forgive.

To win the person, we might have to lose the argument.

The entire time we hold onto this unforgiveness, our heart is closed. We miss opportunities to minister to people around us because our minds are focused on ourselves. While we guard our own hearts, we can't heal anyone else's. Walk with the attitude of forgiveness. Free yourself from that prison and set your heart free to continue to love other people.

Take care to guard not only your heart but also your actions. When people wrong us, our natural reaction might be to get even or settle the score. The natural, fleshly response is to retaliate. We will be tempted to vindicate ourselves. If this person has given information we can prove false, the desire to expose them or simply "tell them off" can be very strong. While it may feel great in the moment to get back at people, it simply deepens the divide in the relationship. The offense will grow, not diminish. Bitterness will sabotage your leadership and close your heart.

It's important to rise above pride and the pain of a wounded spirit to see the bigger picture. Do we want to be proven right or would we rather be right with the person? Sometimes we have to swallow our pride so we don't terminate the relationship. To win the person, we may have to lose the argument. If we're always fighting to be proven right, it not only fractures the relationship, it reveals something about where we find our security and identity. Set your pride aside and do what's best for them, not just for you. Getting even is actually not really possible. You may settle the score, but you will sever the relationship.

This is why many people leave churches. There is unresolved conflict. Hearts are closed. Relationships become forced, tense, and awkward. Rather than have the difficult conversations that would clear the air, many people choose simply to move down the road. They find a place to start new relationships rather than deal with the problems in the established ones.

Conflict remains unresolved simply because someone refuses to forgive. People dig their heels in, refusing to yield ground. They think somehow that they lose if they concede. Yet without reconciliation, *everyone* loses. We lose a friend, the church loses a family member, and we lose out in our relationship with God.

It often seems as if it would be easier to ignore the elephant in the room or to sweep the conflict under the rug. We think that if we say nothing the problem will simply disappear. This is true because the problem is a person, and if we don't deal with the problem, the person will disappear–out of our church, out of our life, and possibly out of Heaven. Always do your best to resolve conflicts. Choose restoration over being right. Lead with an open heart. Forgive.

Forgiveness isn't forgetting. It is refusing to demand payment for the debt that is owed.

Take the Highest Road

Pastor Don Nordin has a saying when dealing with people in relationships. He says, "Don't take the high road; take the highest road." When people mistreat or misunderstand you, don't respond in kind. Let your response be much better than anyone would expect.

Romans 12:17 says, *"Do not repay anyone evil for evil. Be careful to do what is right in the eyes of everyone."* This verse reminds me of time I was caught responding to bullies on the playground. It seemed like there was never a teacher, principal, or anyone around when the bully was attacking me, calling me chubby, or making fun of my "husky" sized pants. I would let the issue go until I boiled over in a rage and responded in kind. It seemed without exception that as I was responding *that's* when an authority would step onto the playground. I would get caught responding. In spite of the fact that they started the fight, I was the one in trouble.

I believe this is a great picture of what Romans 12:17 is saying–to "do what is right in the eyes of everyone." Instead of returning evil for evil, we should take the highest road. We should be careful to do what is right in the eyes of everyone. In other words, if people see only our *response* to what is done to us, they would judge us as righteous, good, and upstanding. On the playground, I returned evil for evil. The principal saw my response and condemned me for it. Had I returned *good* for evil, he would have commended me for it.

We must measure our responses. When someone lashes out or attacks us, we have to take care that our response is what is good, not what is evil.

Recently my son Hunter went to a birthday party. People posted pictures of the party on social media. Hunter received malicious and angry texts from one of the students he had been leading and discipling. He felt as though my son had intentionally excluded him from the party even though Hunter had nothing to do with who was and was not invited. Hunter's first response was anger. He had done all he could over the past weeks to demonstrate unconditional love and acceptance to this student. I coached Hunter through his response; I told him he had to take the highest road. This student's perception and reality didn't align. Even though it would have felt good for Hunter to come back over the top with his responses, defending himself, and putting the other person in his place, it would have cost him his leadership.

I walked my son through the steps of restoring that relationship. I cautioned my son neither to expose the person to someone else nor to lash out at the one who attacked his character. I urged him to make a phone call and work through the issue with this teenager. He did. He took the highest road. The relationship is restored, and this young man is receiving ministry and healing from the rejection he felt so deeply.

It's very easy to become cynical and bitter regarding loving broken people. The old saying "Hurt people hurt people" is true. Keeping your relationship with Jesus a high priority will keep your identity from being formed by the opinions of others.

If you're going to become a Second Mile Leader, you'll have many of these situations happen throughout your ministry. It's important to have a controlled and measured response when these things happen. It's easy to respond in the same way you're being treated, but it's not beneficial. Take the highest road.

**We tend to judge ourselves by our motives,
but others by their actions.**

Have An Open Heart

If you've ever heard someone say "I can forgive, but I won't forget," what that usually means is that person actually *won't* forgive.

We really never forget the things that happen to us. Whether it is a betrayal or abuse, the memories of those moments will always be with us. If you haven't forgotten a trauma, you're not alone. Forgiveness isn't forgetting. It is refusing to demand payment for the debt that is owed. It's refusing to try to collect the debt from the person.

Of course we need wisdom to establish boundaries where necessary to keep the hurt and pain from happening again, but we also need to be able to open our hearts to restored relationships. Many people refuse to allow others back into relationship if they ever do something that offends them. While it's understandable, it's not like Christ. We have to allow people to restore the relationship and move past the old wounds.

When people return to the relationship seeking restoration, our response is critical. We need to be big enough people to allow them to receive it and return. We should not make them jump through hoops or hold them at arm's length. We should not embarrass or humiliate them. Instead we should allow people to return and keep their dignity. Our ability to allow people back into the circle of trust speaks volumes regarding the type of leader we are. Giving grace to those humbling themselves is a demonstration of the character of God. The best leaders have the ability to restore people into relationship.

Just because this is noble does not mean it is easy. It can be very difficult to allow people back into relationship when they walked away, especially if they did it while hurting or humiliating you. Everything in you will want to keep them away or make them undergo some form of penance.

I admit this one is difficult for me. I'm with George W. Bush on this one who said, "Fool me once, shame on you. Fool me twice ...

see, you can't get fooled again." I'm with the movie character Madea who says, "When people show you who they are, *believe* them." In other words, I'd rather just move on, protect myself, and walk away from people who will most likely hurt me again. But Jesus asks me to keep my heart open.

Pastor Don Nordin excels at this. He is one of the most gracious and loving people I know. It seems he gives people 1000 chances. Even when they leave saying negative things about him, he allows them to return and be restored. I've watched him open his arms to people I know have stabbed him in the back many times over. He continues to keep an open heart.

The goal of leading with an open heart is to lead in such a way that the person can be restored in relationship–first to God, then to other believers. If they cannot be restored to us, however, it is possible they will never be restored to God. While we might prefer they find another leader or friend, God may be asking us to walk them personally to freedom. Keep an open heart.

Give The Benefit Of The Doubt

We tend to judge ourselves by our motives, but others by their actions. If we misspeak or act in a way that might hurt others, we give ourselves a pass. We tell ourselves it's OK because "I didn't mean it that way."

Yet if people respond poorly toward us, we look no deeper than their actions. We assume their motives are bad. We do not ask ourselves if this is their typical behavior. We don't consider this moment against the backdrop of their history. We don't look for a reason to excuse their behavior; we look for a way to hold them accountable. They acted poorly; they should pay. All this happens as we are giving ourselves a pass on our own behavior.

People will try to live up to a reputation you claim they have.

One of my former pastors called me one day and chastised me for a mistake over which I had no control. He was extremely angry (nearly in a rage). His correction was way out of control and way out of proportion to the mistake that was made.

I was so caught off guard, I responded in kind. I became very hostile in my response. I was actually lucky to keep my job. In the moment, I never stopped to consider the pastor's character or history. This was so unlike him. Why was his response so different than normal? Where was all this anger coming from?

Had I taken a breath, I might have remembered that he was fighting an infection and had just been prescribed a very strong steroid. He was walking around constantly hopped up on 'roids and had a chip on his shoulder. The chemicals were altering his brain chemistry. Had I stopped to consider this, the call might have been humorous instead of nearly job-ending.

Let's face it. We don't like to give people the benefit of the doubt. Even though they are characterized by being kind, we prefer to throw them away over a single act. We don't consider that they might be having a bad day, going through a struggle, or simply misspeaking in the situation.

In the American courtrooms we are considered innocent until proven guilty. Public opinion may be that the defendant is guilty, but the burden is on the State to prove it beyond a reasonable doubt. Many times in relationships we take the opposite position. We often decide people are guilty until they can prove themselves innocent.

This is a definitive indicator that our hearts are full of suspicion, fear, and doubt. It is very difficult, if not impossible, to lead others when your opinion of them is low. You would do well to speak of people in terms of what you would love to see them become. In Dale Carnegie's classic book *How To Win Friends and Influence People,* he makes this statement about people: "Give them a fine reputation to live up to, and they will make prodigious efforts rather than see you disillusioned."[17] You'd be surprised just how hard people will try to live up to a reputation you claim they have. Have a high opinion of the people God has given you to lead. Believe they can become all God intends for them to be. Speak to their potential instead of their problems. Believe in them. Give people grace. Give them the benefit of the doubt. You just might be surprised at what happens when you do.

Trade Your Rights For Responsibilities

In this country we are conditioned to the idea that we have rights. We have a Bill of Rights entitling us to certain things as individuals. I am personally thankful for the Bill of Rights. Without it, our freedoms would constantly be in jeopardy.

It seems, however, that there is something sinister in our society that extends far beyond our rights. We live in a generation in which many people feel entitled. They feel that they deserve certain levels of care, compensation, respect, and honor regardless of what they have done to merit them.

While there is nothing wrong with having rights, there is something evil about entitlement. Sadly this entitlement mentality has found its way into the church as well. People feel certain things should be done for them and provided for them. They demand preference for their opinions or desires.

**Law forcefully limits my liberty;
love willingly limits my liberty.**

Biblical leadership demands that we trade rights for responsibilities. Jesus modeled it. Paul reiterated it in 1 Corinthians in which he expressed his right to eat whatever his conscience allowed. He asserted that it was not a sin for him to consume meat even if it had been used in ceremonies honoring pagan idols. He could do it if he so chose. It would not affect his relationship with God.

Paul *also* said, however, that there was a bigger issue in play here. Even though he was within his rights to eat this meat, he realized someone who was weaker in his faith might assume he was worshipping the idols. That person might then be led into pagan idolatry through Paul's exercise of his rights. Paul's right might lead them to wrong. So Paul stated that even though he had this right, he was willing to lay it down for the benefit of his brother with a weaker conscience. He said,

> Be careful, however, **that the exercise of your rights** does not become a stumbling block to the weak.

When you sin against them in this way and wound their weak conscience, you sin against Christ. Therefore, if what I eat causes my brother or sister to fall into sin, I will never eat meat again, so that I will not cause them to fall. (1 Corinthians 8:9,12-13 NIV)

Paul said he would give anything up that would cause his brother or sister to fall into sin. Are you willing to do that? This is a hard question for an American. We are so used to being told all the things we deserve. We believe there are many things we are entitled to have. This is reinforced for people of all ages. We give our children trophies in sports simply because they participated, regardless of what they achieved. In every way we continue to reinforce the idea of entitlement without responsibility.

But Paul is saying that while the law is fair, love is sacrificial. The law makes sure everyone gets what he is entitled to. The same rights extend to all people. Love, instead, chooses to be sacrificial. Law *forcefully* limits my liberty; love *willingly* limits my liberty! Love focuses on the object, not itself, and it is perfectly fine trading its rights for responsibilities.

Choose To Love

When it comes down to it, we must *choose* to love. Our relationships with others may not be blissful. They may be a struggle. It may be hard to love those inside the church and even harder to love a society that doesn't know Jesus or appreciate His love.

But the church isn't to be an inward-focused organization

that has no concern for those outside its walls. It is meant to be a force in the world that repels the darkness. Jesus said the gates of Hell won't prevail against the church. The church is to be in active pursuit of destroying every place Hell has an established realm of authority. We are to push back the gates and liberate the lives of the ones Jesus loves.

To prevail against Hell, we have to do what Jesus did. We have to go after sick people. The big surprise is that the sick aren't only outside the church. There are plenty of saints still dealing with sickness. As leaders we are responsible to treat the sick. As we do, we are going to be exposed to those sicknesses. Yet if we put on the right protection for our hearts, we can help others without being hurt in the process. It's time for us to step willfully into painful situations because we love as Jesus loved. John tells us that the litmus test of whether we know God or not is if we love others.

> But anyone who does not love does not know God, for
> God is love. (1 John 4:8 NLT)

To love God means to love other believers and to love the world. The only way we can do that is to lead with an open heart. We risk exposure and we risk injury when we love others, but we can have the protection that keeps our heart open and free from being hurt. So how do we keep ourselves protected as we minister to others?

Forgive. Take the highest road. Have an open heart. Give the benefit of the doubt. Trade your rights for responsibilities. Choose to love.

LEAD WITH AN OPEN HEART.

15

ARE YOU FAT?

The difference between winning and losing
is most often not quitting.
- Walt Disney

There are three things you never ask a woman: How old are you? How much do you weigh? When is the baby due? These questions will land you in hot water. They are so risky that you need a medical license in order to get away with asking them. For common folk like you and me, it's best simply to steer clear of these questions.

But today I'm going to ask you, whether you're a man or a woman: Are you fat? Now before you get offended, remember that if you're in the chubby group like me, you're not alone. The likelihood of you being a bit overweight is fairly high if you live in the United States. We love to eat. In fact, eating is my favorite hobby. If you ask me if I'm hungry, my answer is usually not "yes" or "no"; it's usually "I could eat." It's as if I'm saying, "I'm not hungry, but since when did that have anything to do with whether we eat or not?"

In the words of the late Chris Farley, "I have what doctors call a little bit of a weight problem." I've had it all my life. When you love food so much, it's hard to keep your weight under control. Remember my politically correct pants I wore as a kid? I was "husky" sized. Nowadays I shop in the "big and tall" section. I've noticed that it's named Big first and Tall second for a reason. Most of the clothes have big as their first priority and tall as their second. A distant third priority it "trendy." Basically putting on a Big and Tall shirt feels a lot like wearing an outdated curtain.

Obviously this chapter isn't about whether or not we are physically fit. It has to do with our leadership character. When I asked you if you're fat, it had nothing to do with the size and shape of your body. Instead it has everything to do with the size and shape of your character. I'm not asking, "Are you fat?" I'm asking, "Are you F.A.T.?" This question has nothing to do with whether or not at your last doctor visit he encouraged you to "lose a few." The question has to do with where you rank in some of the most critical character points of a future Second Mile Leader. Are you F.A.T.?– FAITHFUL, AVAILABLE, TEACHABLE.

There are certainly many points of your emotional and spiritual health that will define whether or not you thrive in your career or leadership, but these three traits, perhaps as much as any other, bear tremendous significance on your ability to be a great leader. Possessing these three character traits as a leader in any realm of church or business is critical.

Without these three traits, you might find doors of opportunity close or perhaps never open to you. Without these you might find yourself wondering why other people who are less qualified than you slip by you in promotions, in leadership, or on the ladder of success. Without being F.A.T., you might find yourself stuck, unable to become the leader that you long to be.

Just as your body needs oxygen to survive, your leadership cannot survive without these traits. Being deficient in these elements will cause you to fail as a leader or to be removed by those who entrusted your position to you. Without these traits, you might simply fade into the background as people no longer want to follow your leadership. Your influence will be lost if you fail in these areas. Leadership dies if the leader is not Faithful, Available, and Teachable.

In Ezekiel God records his desire to find a man who will be a leader and protector for the nation of Israel:

*So **I sought for a man** among them who would make a wall, and stand in the gap before Me on behalf of the land, that I should not destroy it; but **I found no one**. (Ezekiel 22:30 NKJV)*

When God has a job to be done, He always starts by choosing and calling an individual. God's plans for the Earth always hinge on finding men and women who will be His instruments of truth, justice, and leadership. It is only when He finds faithful, available, and teachable people on the Earth that the land is preserved, lives are saved, and the purpose of God prevails. I believe as you're reading this now, you have been feeling God's Spirit tugging on your heart to become someone who can stand in the gap between man and God–to go forward as a Second Mile Leader, restoring the purpose and plan of God in the lives of the people in the world. God needs us to be people he can trust–people who are Faithful, Available and Teachable.

FAITHFUL

As Paul is establishing Timothy, a faithful son in leadership, he gives him guidance on how to establish the next generation of leadership that is coming behind him:

> *The things that you have heard from me among many witnesses,* **commit these to faithful men** *who will be able to teach others also. (2 Timothy 2:2 NKJV)*

Notice Paul's priority for selection of leaders. He does not tell tell Timothy to commit his teachings to talented men, influential men, or to wealthy men. Paul doesn't tell Timothy to pick the men who can really wow people with their persuasive speech and colorful illustrations. He doesn't tell him to look for men who are popular or can make people laugh. His thought is not to look for men who are connected to the the movers and shakers in the city–people who can garner enough political clout to sway the church or the city council. He doesn't consider the giving records of each church member, ensuring that people who give the most are placed in positions of prominence. None of these considerations are made.

Instead Paul tells Timothy to entrust his teaching to **faithful** men. He urges Timothy to be careful in his selection. He wants him to pick men that are reliable, men who commit and follow through, men of character and integrity.

**Many people are willing to commit but are
unwilling to pay the price to follow through.**

From the time I arrived at the church I now lead, I began looking for people who could pass the F.A.T. test. These are the people I want to give my life to. They are the ones who can be counted on, week after week. They are the ones who will be faithful to carry the vision forward.

The same is true for you at your job or in your church. Your pastor or boss is looking for someone who has some inward resolve to follow through and do what they say, not someone who commits today and walks out tomorrow.

Proverbs says it like this, *"Many claim to have unfailing love, but a faithful person who can find? (Proverbs 20:6 NIV).* The truth is that many people are willing to commit but are unwilling to pay the price to follow through. You have certainly found this to be true in your own life. People will tell you to your face that they will help you with a task or a project but are nowhere to be found when it is time to do the heavy lifting. If you text them a reminder, they offer up some excuse of an emergency that has come up or previous commitment they had forgotten when they promised you.

This is unfaithfulness. The Bible says a righteous man swears to his own hurt (Psalm 15:4). When we make commitments, we should be people who follow through with those commitments no matter the cost to us financially, emotionally, or physically. If you say you will show up, then show up.

When we take on the responsibility of an area of ministry, a task, or a group of people, we need to understand the full extent of our commitment prior to saying yes. When we do, it should become non-negotiable for us to follow through at or above the level of commitment we made to the project or people. To do less is to be unfaithful.

The dictionary defines the word faithful as "strict or thorough in the performance of duty, and [being] true to one's word, promises, vows, etc." Ask yourself if this describes you. Do you follow through no matter what?

God spoke of a day when He would have servants in His ministry who would be faithful. He said, "Then I will raise up a **faithful** priest who will serve me and do what I desire. I will establish his family, and **they will be priests to my anointed kings forever** (1 Samuel 2:35 NLT). God said the kind of priest He wanted to have was one that was faithful; furthermore, He pointed to faithfulness as the key to the longevity of their leadership.

God is looking for people who will be faithful. He describes faithfulness as those who are willing to continue in service; they don't just stop and start. They have a heart of a servant. They don't view their service as something they do because the pastor asked. They see their service as their response to God and His faithfulness. They are serving Him, not man.

God says they will do what He desires. A faithful servant to God is one that knows what he is doing fulfills God's desire on the

Earth. Faithfulness isn't us promoting our own desire or ministry. It isn't creating a platform or a voice of influence so others will look at us. Faithful service brings God's kingdom to Earth.

God says they will be His forever. When we accept positions of leadership or serving, we should not do so with a plan to take the quickest exit as soon as possible. We should not see it as a stepping stone to some other ministry or program. The roles we take as leaders, whether large or small, require our full attention and devotion. Be faithful where you lead. Have a long-term view and develop a long-term strategy. This is the heart of faithfulness.

The leader who is seeking to entrust you to a position of leadership has several questions regarding your faithfulness. Will you be faithful to the ministry? Will you own it as though it is your own? Will you make sure it is taken care of if you're out of town? Will you do it even when you don't feel like it? Will you continue when the new has worn off and your 'get to' becomes a 'have to?' When you desire to move to a new area of ministry, will you raise up your replacement?

1 Corinthians 4:2 says, *"Now, a person who is put in charge as a manager must be faithful."* This is the first part of the F.A.T. test. Are you Faithful?

God should get our best, not our leftovers.

AVAILABLE

I have served in ministry many years and have watched people, who have desperately wanted a paid position on the church team, be passed over multiple times because they failed the availability test. When the moment came to bring a paid person on the team, they had walked away through discouragement or distraction. Because they were no longer around, a person that might have been much less qualified or served for less time was picked for the position. The reason? They were there. They were **available**.

The subsequent conversation with the person who had walked away and then felt slighted and passed over was as predictable as it was sad. They would ask why had they been passed over when they had served previously. It was simply a matter of availability. It is the nature of leadership to pick the person who is engaged at the moment when the moment of opportunity arises.

This is why it is important to remain faithful **and** available. While the person had previously made himself available, he walked away for some reason. He was not serving at the opportune time. Questions regarding his future faithfulness are overshadowed by the lack of commitment at the moment. Can he regain his faithfulness? Will he recommit? What is going on to make him fall away in this moment? With a cloud of doubt hovering over the person, the offer typically went to the person who had made himself available at the time.

This principle is so clearly illustrated in the story of Elijah and Elisha. The younger had served the older faithfully. He could not have made a higher commitment of faithfulness and availability. He walked away from his career. He abandoned his family. His commitment certainly could not have been challenged, but it was.

As Elijah was nearing the end of his ministry, he tried to get Elisha to leave him. I believe he was giving him the availability test. He told him to "wait here." Elisha would not have it. He told him there was no way he would leave him.

I personally believe this test was not necessary. After all, hadn't Elisha already proven these things to his master? He had walked away from everything! Yet Elijah continued to put him to the test.

Finally, when the end was upon him, Elijah asked Elisha what he wanted as an inheritance for his loyal service. Elisha asked for a **double** anointing. Watch what Elijah said was necessary for Elisha to get what he wanted:

"You have asked a difficult thing," Elijah replied. "If you see me when I am taken from you, then you will get your request. But if not, then you won't." (2 Kings 2:10 NLT)

Elijah told Elisha he could have his request if he was with him at the end–if he remained *available*. "If you are near me when the end comes, you will have it. If you are here at the transition, you will get what you want. If not, you won't."

Are you being passed over time after time because you don't stay until the time of transition? Have you seen someone step in as you stepped out of a position of ministry and within only a few weeks be chosen for the position you wanted? The truth is that they inherited what you worked so hard for. Perhaps it happened because you were not available until the end.

Availability is also key to training. Training leads to promotion into positions. This is illustrated through Samuel's life. God called out to Samuel, attempting to raise him up as a minister. When Eli finally explained what Samuel was hearing, look at His response:

And the LORD came and called as before, "Samuel! Samuel!" And Samuel replied, "Speak, your servant is listening." (1 Samuel 3:10 NLT)

Samuel was saying, "I'm here. I'm ready. I'm willing. I am available." This is key. You and I must be willing to listen to the Lord, but also to listen to the Lord through our leaders. God has appointed them over ministry and placed them in the role of spiritual authority. When those leaders call us out to positions of service, we have to choose to make ourselves available.

When I finally fully surrendered my life to God at 14, I immediately felt the call of God on my life to full-time ministry. As I said in an earlier chapter, I reordered my life around this desire. I kept showing up. When an opportunity came for me to join a paid staff, I was chosen–not because I was best and brightest but because I was available. My youth pastor had confidence in me that I was trustworthy. He was willing to put his own reputation on the line because I had proven myself to be someone he could trust.

Never underestimate the power of availability. Whether it is in your career or in an opportunity to serve in the church, the person who will be picked is the one who is available at the time and has a history of being faithful. This is more than just physical presence. It also has to do with our attitude when we are asked to take on a project and our willingness to say yes. Your boss, your leader, your pastor is looking for someone they don't have to beg in order to shoulder responsibility or take on a project. They want someone who is looking to do more and be more. They want someone who is not looking to do the minimum but is willing to do what it takes. Isaiah demonstrated this heart:

> Then I heard the Lord asking, "Whom should I send as a messenger to this people? Who will go for us?" I said, "Here I am. Send me." (Isaiah 6:8 NLT)

God is looking for people to say, "Here I am. Send me." A person who voluntarily makes himself available is much easier to use than someone who must be poked and prodded. We must arrange our priorities and schedules around the call of God on our lives. Little can be done with someone who is unwilling or unable to make himself available.

In order to lead in God's Kingdom, we must make the things of God a priority in our lives. This means we will likely need to adjust our schedule. We may need to give up some leisure. We might need to forego some trips or "me" time.

If you are still reading this book at this point, you are probably convinced that the church is the physical representation of God's Kingdom and is the ultimate pursuit on Earth. If you believe this, you probably have the sense that God wants us to reorder or lives around it. God's purpose in our lives is expressed as a part of the local church and the family of God it represents. We need to become people who make its work and the relationships in it a priority in our lives. We need to be people who give the church our first, not our last. God should get our best, not our leftovers. We need to be people that say I'm ready and willing. As Isaiah said, we say, "Pick me. Send me." We need to become people who say whatever, wherever, whenever, I'm ready and willing to be used by God for His purpose and plan in the Earth.

Many people have talent and character, but they simply will not or cannot make themselves available. This was a case I found several times in one of the ministries I was leading. I had a person who was extremely talented. His hobby was the same as the ministry I oversaw. What he did in his spare time for fun was what I needed him to do in the church for ministry. It was a perfect fit, but the only time this man would talk to me about being a part of my team was when he was looking for me to hire him to be a part of it. The irony was stunning. Why would I pay a person to lead a team made up entirely of volunteers but who would never volunteer himself?

If you're called to do ministry as part of the paid staff at a church, you need to understand that you will likely spend several years proving that calling as an unpaid staff member. This is no different than those who seek a career in a medical field who do unpaid internships. This is the proving ground.

If you're not called to fulfill your ministry in life as part of the paid staff of a church, however, it's likely that you will be a permanent volunteer. This is because ministry isn't something we are paid to do. Ministry is something we are called to do. We are paid so we can do ministry, not paid to do ministry. It really bothers me when I find people who want to serve in the church, but their first question concerns how much they will be paid. Your pastor is likely not looking for someone who wants a job. They are most likely looking for someone to own the vision.

Many people who serve in our church cannot afford to quit their jobs. I simply could not pay them at the level of income they receive through their careers, yet they serve at a high level of availability. They are sold out to the cause of Christ in the world. I can't buy them. I can't pay them to do ministry. They serve because they own the vision.

From time to time, people will talk about coming to the church during the day to work as a volunteer. They ask, "If I come, what would you want me to do?" The honest answer is that I don't know. I tell them to just show up and continue showing up. I don't know what will need to be done on whatever day they decide to show up. I also don't know what they are capable of doing or if I will have something to match their skill sets. Finally I do not know if this person is going to follow through and really make himself available. Leaders will invest themselves only in people who continue to make themselves available. It is not worth the effort to train someone to do a complex task if he is unwilling to continue to do it.

If they will show up and keep showing up, they will find themselves with more to do than they can possibly get done. If they continue to make themselves available, they will be promoted in leadership positions (paid or unpaid) because they continue to be trained and become more useful. Availability produces capability.

People sometimes ask me why a certain person is leading an area. They want to know why they get the microphone, why they are calling the shots. The answer is seldom that they are more qualified. The answer is usually that they continued to make themselves available. They just kept showing up.

Future pastors and leaders, do not ask your leader to make a spot for you so you will show up. Show up, and they will make a spot for you. Make yourself indispensable, and you will find yourself in the position or job. In the world of careers, this translates into "Do the job before you get paid for it and at some point, you will get paid for it."

I would rather train and correct a Faithful and Available person than to use a super-talented one who wants in it for what he can get out of it. In the beginning, he might have been the least qualified person to lead or talk, but because he kept showing up, he acquired the skills necessary to do the job effectively.

You must be available, or the organization will simply move on past you. New leaders emerge. New faces show up. As the organizational makeup changes, your leadership fades. Make yourself available.

When we stop learning, we stop leading.

TEACHABLE

The third characteristic we must have to pass the FAT test is to be teachable. We should understand that we just don't know all we need to know.

Aristotle said it like this: "The more you know, the more you know you don't know." The more you learn about life, leadership, and love, the more you realize you have so much more to learn. The hidden implication here is that the *less* we know the more we think we know. Our confidence is higher when our ignorance is greater. The only way we can really continually maintain a teachable attitude is to walk in humility and seek out coaching, mentoring, and training.

Leaders are learners. When we stop learning, we stop leading. We will never know all we need to know until we reach perfection itself–Heaven, so we must never stop learning.

Learning requires a teachable spirit. This is where many of us fail the test. We allow a little success or knowledge to puff us up. Pride gets in the way of our ability to learn from others. If someone points out a way our idea could be better, we protect it instead of allowing it to be improved. If someone coaches, corrects, or confronts us, we react and push back. We might be faithful and available, but not teachable. This stifles our growth and stops our forward movement.

Ralph Waldo Emerson said, "Every man I meet is my superior in some way, and in that I learn from him." If we can have a teachable spirit, we can learn from anyone. People can help us grow even if they are not an expert in our field. Simply having an outside perspective can show us things that we would otherwise not see.

A few weeks ago our team attended a leadership conference.

The speaker was a dynamic and engaging communicator. During his presentation, he talked about the importance of having a coach to help you get better at your craft. He said the person who coached him was present in the audience and would be speaking during the following session.

Naturally when this "coach" got up to speak, I expected him to be on a level two or three steps above this communicator who claimed him as his coach. He wasn't. In fact he wasn't very good at all. I was confused at first; then it hit me. A person doesn't have to be *better* than you to give you coaching and advice. He simply needs a different perspective than you. The ability to see from outside your situation can help you improve things you never would have thought to change.

Jesus was able to use the disciples not only because they were faithful and available but also because they were teachable. They blundered over and over. Each time, Jesus would correct them and set them back on course.

Being teachable means we are willing to submit ourselves to instruction from people and leaders around us. Trust me; those around you see blind spots in your leadership. This does not mean that you are a bad leader; however, lacking the humility to learn from those around *does* make you a bad leader. Without humility, you will never grow.

Your leadership will be capped. Those who placed you in leadership will replace you with someone who is teachable. People you lead will become frustrated and move to another leader because you are unwilling to accept their input or suggestions. Mark Twain once said, "Never undertake to instruct a pig to sing. You'll only frustrate yourself and annoy the pig." Don't be a pig. Be teachable.

Here's a short litmus test. I challenge you to sit and reflect on these questions. If you are really bold and want to grow as a leader, find someone and ask them to answer these questions about you honestly:

Are you someone who thinks he doesn't need to be taught? When was the last time you sought out training or perspectives for your area other than your own?

Are you someone who refuses to be taught? Do you reject input and constructive criticism from others?

Are you someone who thinks he arc too old to learn new things? Have you given up on pushing ahead for another season?

Paul talks about a group of people that has a mental block when it comes to growth in their relationship with God. I believe it also applies to our leadership ability. He described them as *"Ever learning, and never able to come to the knowledge of the truth"* (2 Timothy 3:7). If we think we are ever going to be able to instruct others, we must be willing to receive instruction!

The writer of Hebrews laments the condition of those he has labored to train and teach. They still have not grown because they listen but do not learn. I love how the Message translation paraphrases this verse:

I have a lot more to say about this, but it is hard to get it across to you since you've picked up this bad habit of not listening. By this time you ought to be teachers yourselves, yet here I find you need someone to sit down with you and go over the basics on God again, starting from square one—baby's milk, when you should have been on solid food long ago! (Hebrews 5:12 MSG)

Many of us should be teachers, but because we never listen, we have never learned anything. Without being teachable, we cannot learn anything valuable to pass on to others. Sometimes we simply do not recognize our own roadblocks to leadership. Being teachable certainly is a large one.

We need to be people who seek out feedback, value the input of others, and seek out coaching and correction. If we realize how valuable feedback can be, we will learn to seek it out and appreciate it. Proverbs says, *"Wounds from a sincere friend are better than many kisses from an enemy." (Proverbs 27:6 NLT).* Learn the gift of seeking out and receiving constructive criticism. It will propel you to the next level.

When we begin to realize that we need to know something we do not yet know, we are at a tipping point of leadership. The breakthrough comes when we respond to that realization by seeking out the perspective and information we need. The more I learn, the more I realize I have to learn. With every step of growth I take, new worlds of wisdom become necessary. I have a vision for our church, but I need the wisdom of those God has given me to help lead me into helping the dream become reality.

Make it easy for those who lead you and those you lead to speak into your leadership. Make it easy for your leader to coach and correct you. Hebrews says,

> *"Obey your spiritual leaders, and do what they say. Their work is to watch over your souls, and they are accountable to God. Give them reason to do this with joy and not with sorrow.* ***That would certainly not be for your benefit.****" (Hebrews 13:17 NLT)*

Making it difficult for our leaders to speak into our lives is not to our benefit. Making it easy certainly is. Make up your mind that you will not wait to be corrected by your leader but that you will seek out the correction and coaching from your leader. Ask him this simple question: "Is there anything in my life and leadership you would like to speak into?" Determine to receive the answer without being offended. This attitude and action will begin to unlock a new level of growth in you.

> *For whoever exalts himself will be humbled, and whoever humbles himself will be exalted."*
> *(Matthew 23:12)*

Being teachable means we have a spirit of humility and a spirit that is eager to grow. Humble yourself and you will be exalted.

Passing the F.A.T. test will propel you to new levels in your ministry or career. Determine to become Faithful, Available, and Teachable.

16

LEADERSHIP COVENANTS

No one ever attains very eminent success by simply doing
what is required of him; it is the amount and excellence of
what is over and above the required that determines the
greatness of ultimate distinction.
- Charles Francis Adams

We have learned about the intention Jesus had for the church, the *ekklésia*. We have learned that we are in the world for God's purposes and not our own. Each one of us is a minister of the grace of Jesus. God is counting on us to fulfill the great commission of making disciples. Now let us look at how we can make that happen.

I believe discipleship happens best in the context of small groups. As I taught this material to our church, my goal was to produce small group leaders. These leaders would help produce other disciples in our church. It is time for you to evaluate if you are ready to take the step of becoming a Second Mile Leader in your congregation for your pastor.

If you are not ready to be a small group leader in your church or if your church does not have a small group ministry, you can still lead at a level that a Second Mile Leader should lead. The Second Mile Leader concept is not exclusive to small group leaders. It is a decision to live to fulfill the purpose of God in this world. It is a commitment of ourselves to the cause of Christ over any other cause. It is our willingness to serve when everyone else has given up and given out. It is a pre-decided "yes" to say to God, "Whatever, wherever, whenever you need me, I'm ready."

While your pastor may be unfamiliar with this book or material, I recommend you review this final chapter and make a decision of whether you are willing to commit to be a Second Mile Leader. If you are, I would suggest to you that after reading the following covenants you print them off, sign them, and present them to your pastor along with your verbal commitment to be a Second Mile Leader in your local church.

I believe that as more and more Christians become this type of leader, we will see the church become the powerful *ekklésia* Jesus left on the Earth. We will experience more than just revival; we will see a spiritual revolution.

Covenants

It is important to make written, clear commitments. The following is a charge for you to live at the same standard of leadership to which Paul challenged Timothy. Making this covenant is an attestation on your part that you are ready and willing to lead and be accountable for that leadership. You are saying, "I want my life to count, I want to be counted on, and I want to be held accountable for my leadership and lifestyle."

Leadership has two important parts. The first is what we will be. The second is what we commit to do. The following is a covenant for what Second Mile Leaders will be and do. There are two: Character and Service.

SECOND MILE LEADERSHIP CHARACTER COVENANT

As an essential part of being a Second Mile Leader, you have a responsibility to develop and exhibit mature Christian behavior. While serving as a Second Mile Leader, you pledge to be presentable in your appearance. You commit to demonstrate Biblical standards in your attire and behavior.

The way we present ourselves as leaders has a great deal of influence on the way people perceive Christ. For this reason, Paul encouraged Timothy to lead by example in order to leverage his influence to lead others toward Christ.

But set an example for the believers in speech, in conduct, in love, in faith and in purity.
(1 Timothy 4:12)

Let's look at the implications for our character and conduct in each of each of these areas.

SPEECH

As a leader in this body, I commit to speak only words that

build others up. I will keep myself from speaking negatively over others and their lives and about this church or its leaders. If I have issues with things that happen in the course of relationships or with the operations of ministries, I will bring those matters to my leaders in private, requesting assistance in providing remedy for the situation.

CONDUCT

I commit to behave in a manner so as to influence people toward Christ, not away. I will seek to live a life that is worthy of imitation. I will conduct myself such that if people follow in my footsteps they will lead them to Jesus.

I realize that as a leader I bear higher responsibility for those around me. I will serve without limits to be as large an influence as possible for the people around me to come to know Christ.

I commit to serving this body of believers. Other than emergencies, vacations, or impacted work schedules, I will seek to be engaged actively in serving and leading the ministry activities of the church.

No area of service is off limits to me. I will serve wherever and whenever and do whatever is needed in order to provide an environment in which others can experience the love and power of Jesus Christ.

LOVE

I commit to exhibiting the characteristics of 1 Corinthians 13 through my life and ministry. I will cover the weaknesses and failings of those in our church family instead of exposing them to others. I will overlook offenses and choose to believe the best about others. I will seek out those who are lonely, hurt, wounded, and broken and pour myself into them. I will believe the best about those in our family and choose to cover their weaknesses and failings instead of exposing them to others.

I commit my life to be a demonstration that I love God by the way I love my brothers and sisters in Christ. I will not gossip about them or slander them. I will take the highest road when opportunities for offense come. I will overlook offenses and choose to believe the best about others.

When necessary, I will lovingly confront others concerning their attitudes and behaviors. I will do this according to Matthew 18. I will go to them privately, confronting them in a manner that will preserve their dignity and draw them back toward Christ.

FAITH

I commit to being a person who is in the Word and prayer daily. I realize that as a leader in this body others will need me to be ready at a moment's notice to pray for and encourage them. My ministry and relationships with others should be a result of the overflow of my relationship with Christ.

People will need to lean on me as a source of strength and hope. It is imperative that my faith is strong and my relationship with God is fresh so I can be a person who lifts the faith of others in their dark hours.

PURITY

I recognize it is not only my visible conduct but also my spiritual condition that influences those I lead. I commit to keep my mind, eyes, and body pure from this world.

According to James 5:16, I will maintain an accountable relationship with a Godly peer in my life to whom I will confess my faults and receive prayer for healing. I commit to have no areas of my life that are off-limits to my accountability partner. I will openly confess my sins, weaknesses, and failures so that I may be healed.

My accountability partner's information:

Name: _____

Phone _____

SECOND MILE LEADERSHIP SERVICE COVENANT

CARE AND CONNECTION

I commit to be a primary connection point for those who are seeking to join our church family. I will seek to provide a welcoming experience to others as they attend for the first time. I will greet guests, learn their names, and invite them to the teams and groups I am leading. I will purposefully sit in the same place weekly and work to create a positive experience for new people, connecting them from the curb to our community. I will assist them in finding a small group and a place to serve.

I will make it easier for our guests and new members to connect to the church. I will park in the farthest spaces necessary and give up my seat in the auditorium as needed. As we move into multiple service times, I will choose the time that needs my presence and leadership the most.

As I meet new people, I will ensure that they complete a guest card and commit to follow up personally with them to get them connected.

LEADERSHIP

I commit to take a lead role or a leadership apprentice role in areas of ministry. I realize that in order for us to grow, we will need more leaders and team members than we currently have. As such, I will always seek to help us staff for growth in every area of ministry. Further, I will seek to train people to serve in whichever position I lead or serve in so that my replacement is always ready and growth is always possible.

CORE BELIEFS

I commit to our church's doctrinal beliefs. I will support our statement of faith both personally and publicly. I will adhere to and practice the same beliefs of our church.

CONTRIBUTION

ATTEND

I commit to making attendance at small groups and week-end services a priority over other activities, hobbies, and interests. I will arrive early and plan to stay late following the services and events.

SERVE

I commit to find ways to demonstrate the love of God through my acts of service. My leadership will rise and fall on my commitment to be a resource to those around me. I will discover and use my specific gifts and talents for the assignments God has given me in the family.

I realize people will follow my example. I can expect them to serve only when I model the behaviors we desire for them to emulate. I will carry the load of ministry of the church through my service.

GIVE

I recognize that it is my responsibility to support the work of God in the world through the resources He has placed in my hands. I commit to give the first 10 percent of my income to support the work of our church family. Additionally I will be obedient to the prompting of the Holy Spirit to give above and beyond my tithe to support the special ministry projects that God places on the heart of our leadership.

ACCOUNTABILITY

Having recognized the importance of spiritual, moral, and ethical accountability, I will seek and receive coaching, correction, and spiritual discipline in my life.

Should I violate any of these covenants, I welcome loving correction in my life. I will humbly and sincerely submit to correction and will seek to remedy a situation or offense for which I am responsible.

Should I fail to submit to the leadership's coaching or correction, I realize it is the right and the duty of spiritual authority to remove me from my position of leadership within this body.

Name: _____

Date: _____

Enduring As Soldiers

As you step into the role of a Second Mile Leader, you should not be surprised when you experience difficulty, resistance, or even offense. The problems we encounter seem normal, natural, and earthly, but much of what happens in the natural is influenced by the spiritual.

We are not fighting people, we are fighting the spiritual influences that want to retain their grip on them (Ephesians 6:12). When we step into their situation as the *ekklésia*, we begin to push back the governments of Hell with the power of God. Although the spirits are defeated, they do fight back. Be prepared. As a person taking up a leadership position, you are moving from the middle of the pack to the front line. You are no longer simply a soldier; you are a commander. As a leader, you become a target for the enemy.

You may experience tension, strain, fatigue, and many other issues. While every problem we face does not have a spiritual origin, many are more spiritual than we give credit. Continue to be a person of prayer. We win the war in the spiritual before we experience victory in the natural.

Our devotion and love for God keeps us in a place of ministry from overflow. Ministering from a deficient relationship with God will allow us to be blindsided easily by the enemy. Never stop praying. Keep your guard up. Stay in accountable relationships.

When it gets hard to keep going, remember that people are counting on you. Quitting is never an option. A war is raging. Eternal lives are at stake.

Never take the easy way out. Keep pressing on in leadership

no matter how hard it gets. As Paul said to Timothy, *"Endure hardship as a good soldier" (2 Timothy 2:3).*

God has asked, "Whom shall I send?" You have answered, "Here am I. Send me." Now it is time to go change the world one conversation at a time, one life at a time, one decision at a time. It is time to plunder Hell and populate Heaven. And when you stand before God, you'll be able to tell Him you never did the minimum. You always did twice what was required because you became a Second Mile Leader.

END NOTES

1   Jenee Woodard, The Abingdon Creative Preaching Annual 2014 (Nashville: Abingdon Press, 2013), 50.

2   Zig Ziglar, See You at the Top (Gretna, LA: Pelican, 2005), 151.

3   Encyclopædia Britannica, "Ecclesia" Web. July 14, 2017.

4   J. Thorley, Athenian Democracy (London: Routledge, 2005), 29-30.

5   Eberhard Bons, Jan Joosten, Regine Hunziker-Rodewald, eds., Biblical Lexicology: Hebrew and Greek: Semantics – Exegesis - Translation (Berlin: Walter de Gruyter, 2015), 279.

6   Lonnie Lane, "Church" Isn't in the New Testament!" last modified September 3, 2009, accessed June 28, 2017, https://sidroth.org/articles/church-isnt-new-testament.

7   David Platt (2010-04-17), Radical: Taking Back Your Faith from the American Dream (New York: Doubleday Religious Publishing Group), Kindle Edition, 7.

8   Ibid., 12.

9   Ibid., 13.

10 Lois Barrett, Missional Church: A Vision for the Sending of the Church in North America (Grand Rapids, MI: William B. Eerdmans Publishing Company), 191-192.

11 https://www.barna.com/research/small-churches-struggle-to-grow-because-of-the-people-they-attract/

12 https://careynieuwhof.com/8-reasons-most-churches-never-break-the-200-attendance-mark/

13 Joel Comiskey, 2000 Years of Small Groups: A History of Cell Ministry in the Church (Lima, OH: CCS Publishing), Kindle Edition, 168-169.

14 D. Michael Henderson, John Wesley's Class Meeting (Nappanee, IN: Evangel Publishing House, 1997), 93.

15 Andy Stanley, Enemies of the Heart: Breaking Free from the Four Emotions That Control You (New York: Crown Publishing Group), Kindle Edition, 159-160.

16 Sam Hinn, William McDowell, "I Give Myself Away," (Delivery Room Publishing, 2008).

17 Dale Carnegie, How To Win Friends and Influence People (New York: Simon & Schuster), Kindle Edition, 252.